The Battle of
Wounded Knee

The Battle of Wounded Knee

The Ghost Dance Uprising

BARBARA BONHAM

Reilly & Lee Books

A DIVISION OF THE HENRY REGNERY COMPANY

Photographs courtesy National Archives, U.S.
Signal Corps. Maps by Walter T. Vitous originally
published in The Last Days of the Sioux Nation,
by Robert M. Utley, copyright © 1963 by
Yale University.

Prologue facing page 1 copyright © 1935 by
The Macmillan Company.

Published 1970 by Reilly & Lee Books
a division of Henry Regnery Company
114 West Illinois Street, Chicago, Illinois 60610
Library of Congress Catalog Card Number 71-125374
Manufactured in the United States of America

CONTENTS

So Hunger throve. And many of the lean,
Who, having eyes for seeing, had not seen,
And, having ears for hearing, had not heard,
Fed hope a little with the wrathful word
And clamored 'round the agencies. "Our
        lands,"
They said, "we sold to you for empty hands
And empty bellies and a white man's lie!
Where is the food we bought? Our children
        die!
The clothing? For our people shiver. Look!
The money for the ponies that you took
Ten snows ago? The Great White Father's
        friends
Have stolen half the little that he sends.
The starving of our babies makes them fat.
We want to tell the Great White Father that.
We cannot live on promises and lies."

—JOHN G. NEIHARDT, *The Song of the Messiah*

1

The Cup of Bitterness

THE TETON Sioux were a broken people. Everything that had
given meaning to their life had been taken from them when
they had been confined to the Great Sioux Reservation in
Dakota Territory in the 1870s.

Once they had been a happy people, roaming over a vast
country, unceasingly active either in war or in the hunt. The
Teton warriors were always on the move and disliked re-
straint. Yet group living required some restriction of individ-
ual desires, and a simple government had evolved over the
centuries to preserve order among the people.

The Sioux Indians were composed of three main groups,
known to the white man as the Santees, the Yanktonais, and
the Tetons. The Indians called themselves the Dakota, Na-
kota, and Lakota, respectively.

The Teton, or Lakota, Sioux consisted of seven tribes:
Oglala, Brule, Hunkpapa, Miniconjou, Sans Arc, Two Kettle,
and Blackfeet. Each of the seven tribes in turn was subdi-
vided into numerous bands that were constantly changing
in size and membership.

Each band had its own chief, but he did not have absolute power over his followers. His duty was to carry out the will of the majority. The chief could influence opinion, but he rarely acted unless most of his followers approved of his course. The rank of chief was either inherited or earned by success in war and strength of character.

There was no single chief who ruled over the entire Teton Sioux nation. During the summer months, all the bands of each of the seven tribes gathered together for a reunion. These gatherings were governed by tribal councils, assisted by deputies and a corps of tribal soldiers.

Among the Oglalas, for example, the governing council consisted of seven band chiefs chosen by the older men of the tribe. The council chose four deputies—young men whose special qualities set them apart from the rest of the tribe. The deputies wore shirts fringed with hair and were called the Shirt Wearers. It was a great honor for a young man of the Oglalas to be selected to be a member of the Shirt Wearers.

The tribal soldiers, or policemen, were chosen from a men's society in each band called the *akicita*. This group kept order in the camp and on moving day. Should an Indian commit the terrible deed of killing a tribesman, the *akicita* put him to death, destroyed all his property, or banished him from the tribe. During the buffalo hunt, when it was important that the hunters follow a plan, the *akicita* saw to it that no one threatened the success of the hunt by pursuing a buffalo independently.

The great herds of bison that ranged the homeland of the Teton Sioux shaped the life of the people. In few other areas of the world did a single animal play so important a role in the culture of a people. Although the Tetons hunted all game animals, it was the buffalo that furnished them with nearly everything they needed in their everyday lives. Buffalo meat was the main item of their diet. Buffalo hide provided material for the Tetons' tepees, clothing, blankets, and for every kind of container. Hooves, horns, and bones were used for

ceremonial objects, cooking utensils, awls, chisels, hide-scrap-
ers, and other tools. Intestines and bladders were used to
carry water. Rope, thread, and bowstrings were made from
buffalo sinews.

Next to hunting, the most important activity of the Sioux
was war. It was through success in battle that a young man
earned prestige, wealth, and high rank. The capture of enemy
scalps required bravery, daring, and cleverness and earned
a young warrior the respect of men and the admiration of
women. Stealing ponies was another objective of war, for the
more ponies a man owned, the more wealthy he was. When a
Sioux warrior wanted to propose marriage, he left as much
personal wealth as he could afford—usually ponies—in front
of the tepee of a girl's father. If the gift was accepted, the
girl moved in with the warrior without further ceremony.
Men of wealth often took several wives, housing them in
different tepees.

Indians showed their children great affection and indulged
their every whim. Rather than discipline their children, Indian parents let their young ones learn from experience.
There were no warnings issued when an Indian baby stuck his
finger toward the fire. If the child burned himself, he learned
the danger of fire in a way he never forgot.

Every thought and activity of the Sioux manifested their
religious beliefs. Living so close to nature, dependent upon
it for survival, the Tetons felt themselves to be a part of
nature. They believed that numerous gods surrounded them.
Wi, the Sun, was the chief god of the Tetons. His virtues were
bravery, fortitude, generosity, and fidelity, and his power was
thought to be obtainable through certain offerings and ceremonies. The most important of the ceremonies was the Sun
Dance, in which a dancer might communicate directly with
Wi. Red symbolized Wi and was the sacred color of all the
Plains Indians. Blue symbolized Skan, the Sky. Green was the
color of Maka, the Earth god, who was the mother of all
things. Inyan, the Rock, was ancestor of all things, even the
gods. His symbolic color was yellow.

There were many other gods, too, including the Moon and the Buffalo gods. All of them merged to become Wakan Tanka, the Great Mysterious, who was everywhere.

All the different kinds of power the Tetons needed were thought to be controlled by the various gods. To become a renowned warrior and hunter, to enjoy a good family life, and to be honored with membership in the men's societies, a Teton had to possess powers that could be obtained only from these gods.

As a Sioux boy stood on the threshold of manhood, he made his first attempt to gain these powers. He went alone into the wilderness, where he fasted, prayed, tortured himself, and waited for a vision to come. When he returned to camp, he went to the medicine man, or shaman, who told him what his vision meant and identified the boy's guardian spirit for life. This spirit might dwell in any object—a bird, an animal, even a bolt of lightning. If the boy's guardian spirit took the form of an eagle or a rabbit, he took care never to harm such a creature and acquired some part of the animal—a feather, an ear, a leg bone—to carry on his person always. This was the Teton's most sacred and valuable possession, for it was the reservoir of his personal power. It would guide and protect him and give him strength throughout his life. Because of their complete faith in their gods and their visions, the Sioux were strong and confident as individuals and as a nation.

In addition to performing religious duties—such as interpreting visions—the shamans functioned as the tribal doctors. As a result of their control of these two important areas, the shamans exerted tremendous power and influence over their people.

Of all the religious ceremonies the Sioux held, the Sun Dance was the most important. The dance took place each summer and lasted eight days. The first four days were devoted to numerous rites and rituals for both men and women. If a man had distinguished himself as a warrior and a leader, he was taken into one of the various societies of the tribe. Feasts were held and gifts exchanged. During the last four days, the actual dance took place. There were four grades of the dance, each demanding a certain amount of discipline and self-torture. Worshipping, supplicating, and communing with the chief god, Wi, were the first three grades of the dance. The fourth grade, danced on the last day, required the greatest amount of self-torture. Most Sioux males danced this fourth grade at least once in their lives. Seldom was it danced more often. The fourth grade of the Sun Dance was a tremendous test of a man's courage and fortitude. Cuts were made in the dancer's breast and a rawhide thong was threaded around his breast and back muscles. The thong was drawn tightly, and the ends were fastened to the top of the dance pole. Then, staring into the face of the sun, often dragging buffalo skulls to increase his weight, the dancer danced around the pole until the thong tore through the flesh of his breast. By practicing this type of self-torture, the warrior hoped to create a personal relationship between himself and Wi, thus securing the Sun god's power for himself and his tribe.

This was the life the Tetons had led before the white men came to take their land. There were simply too many of the whites. Their guns were too big, their armies too strong. One by one the Teton bands yielded to the urging of the Great Father in Washington and gave up their old free life for a life of safety from the soldiers' guns and for the promise of food in the days of the vanishing buffalo herds. Some of the Tetons were stubborn and held out. But in 1877, with the surrender of the last two hostile chiefs, Sitting Bull and Crazy Horse, the Sioux settled down resignedly to reservation life.

The Great Sioux Reservation, which was all the land the Sioux could still claim as their own, was bounded on the east by the Missouri River, on the south by the Nebraska line, on the north by the present line between North and South Dakota, and on the west by the Black Hills. This area was owned by all seven tribes of the Teton Sioux. Each tribe was assigned to an agency, where they were to receive their rations and from which they were ruled by government-appointed agents, many of whom used their authority to establish their own small empires. To enforce their orders, the agents recruited a number of Indians to serve as policemen.

Red Cloud's Oglala Sioux, numbering about seventy-three hundred, and five hundred Northern Cheyennes, under Little Chief, were assigned to the Pine Ridge Agency. The Cheyennes had been neighbors of the Sioux on the high plains for generations but had been moved to Indian Territory in the southwestern United States by the white government. Ultimately, Little Chief had arranged for the return of his band to their northern home. Four thousand Brules, under Spotted Tail, were assigned to the Rosebud Agency. These two agencies—Pine Ridge and Rosebud—lay about sixty miles apart, just north of the Nebraska line. Up the Missouri from the Rosebud, about one thousand Lower Brules lived at their agency, and another thousand Lower Yanktonais were across the river at Crow Creek. Still farther north along the Missouri was the Cheyenne River Agency, home of some three thousand Miniconjou, Blackfeet, Sans Arc, and Two Kettle Sioux. At Standing Rock, the northernmost agency along the Missouri, about seventeen hundred Hunkpapa, Blackfeet, and Upper Yanktonai Sioux were enrolled. In all, the Teton Sioux on the reservation numbered close to sixteen thousand.

Once the Sioux were confined to the reservation, the white men began to pull apart, thread by thread, the rich fabric of the old Sioux life. The United States government set out to civilize the Sioux. It expected the Indians to make the jump overnight from the Stone Age to the modern era, a change that had taken the white man centuries to accomplish. As a first step, the government was determined to turn the Sioux into God-fearing, hard-working tillers of the soil. Such a change would have been enormously difficult for a primitive, nomadic people to make under any circumstances. For the Sioux it was particularly upsetting. Under the government plan, they were forced to give up all warfare, by which a Teton warrior proved himself a man. In place of this major activity, the Indians were expected to take up an occupation they considered demeaning. The Sioux had always looked upon farmers as inferior beings, men without the skills or bravery to live by war and the hunt.

The Sioux were no longer permitted to hunt the buffalo. This restriction was imposed, not only because officials in Washington regarded the annual hunt as barbaric, but because the buffalo was growing scarce. At first the Sioux tried to recapture the excitement of the hunt by killing the cattle they were issued as rations in the same manner as they had once killed the buffalo. But many white officials believed that this would only serve to keep alive the so-called savage instincts of the people they were trying to civilize, and so after two years the Indian Bureau stopped the practice.

Deprived of their major source of food, the buffalo, the Sioux became almost completely dependent upon the white government for all their material needs. The staple of their diet became low-grade beef. One bony steer was expected to feed as many as thirty people over a two-week period. In addition to beef, the Indians were issued green coffee beans, coarse brown sugar, and wormy flour of a quality no white family would have used. Several treaties and agreements between the United States government and the Sioux nation promised rations to the Indians until they became self-supporting. When an Indian proved he had learned enough about farming to take care of himself and his family, he was to be given 160 acres of his own. Once an Indian established himself on his own farm, rations would no longer be issued to him.

In order to hasten the day when the Sioux would be self-supporting, the agents on the reservations were instructed to break up the camps and encourage the Indians to scatter and settle on plots that they could farm. The Indian Bureau furnished the necessary seeds and implements, as well as breeding stock for cattle herds.

At first the program made little progress. The Sioux could not be convinced that farming was respectable work for a man, although they found herding beef cattle more to their liking. Those Indians who yielded to the agents' urging and began to work the fields suffered the scorn of their fellow tribesmen.

Through the 1880s, however, more and more of the Sioux gave in and began to scatter over the reservation, building cabins (which they disliked as dwellings), breaking the sod, and planting just enough seed to satisfy the agents. But they found living in one place depressing, and more often than not, they would move at the end of the season to be closer to friends or relatives. The work of building and plowing would then have to be done over again.

There existed an even greater obstacle to the success of the Sioux as farmers than their attitude and wanderlust. Neither the soil nor the climate on the reservation was conducive to farming. There were several good years, but in the latter half of the 1880s, drought, grasshoppers, hail, and hot winds caused the crops to fail. Agent Charles E. McChesney of the Cheyenne River Agency flatly told the Indian Bureau in 1887 that the area was not fit for farming. Everyone at the bureau was so determined to turn the Indians into farmers, however, that no one listened to the agent.

It was believed in Washington—and rightly—that education of the Indian children would be the most important step toward bringing about the absorption of the Sioux into the mainstream of American society. To this end, day schools on the reservation and several boarding schools scattered throughout the United States were founded. Although Indian parents suffered great anguish at being separated from their children, agents compelled attendance at these schools by withholding rations from Indian fathers who refused to co-operate.

After a time, boarding schools were built on the reservation itself, and parents were less reluctant to send their children. But it soon became apparent to the Sioux that their children were being subjected to a stern discipline unknown at home and were being weaned away from values that the Indians cherished.

On the first day of school at the Pine Ridge Agency, a crowd of Indians gathered. The children disappeared inside the schoolhouse, and the teachers drew the blinds. But a breeze blew the blinds aside, and a father saw one teacher holding his son while another snipped off the boy's long, braided hair, symbol of Sioux manhood. The crowd stormed the school and rescued the children.

But by the closing years of the 1880s, the Sioux had been forced to surrender their children to the schools. Their resentment toward the whites increased.

An attack was made by the whites on the government of the Sioux, as well. Instructions were issued to the agents from the Indian Bureau to destroy the authority of those chiefs who resisted the changes the white men were forcing upon the Sioux. When a chief advised his followers to disobey the commands of their agent, some agents did not hesitate to withhold rations or send out the agency police force to compel obedience. When threatened with hunger or arrest, most tribal councils withdrew their support from a rebellious chief. The result was confusion. With their leaders discredited, the Indian people did not know where to look for guidance.

The religion of the Sioux also came under attack. In order to root out paganism among the Indians and turn them into Christians, the white men forbade the Sioux to continue many of the customs they had followed for centuries. A list of Indian "offenses" was issued to the agents with orders to prevent their practice. Among the offenses were having more than one wife, purchasing a wife by leaving ponies at her father's door, all practices of medicine men, and holding feasts and dances. The restriction of their feasts and dances struck at the heart of the spiritual life of the Sioux. Many of the dances were social and were held purely for entertainment. They were held frequently and were the source of much enjoyment. Others were religious, and of these, as has been noted, the Sun Dance was of supreme importance. During the eight emotion-charged days of the dance, all the values and beliefs the tribe lived by were emphasized and dramatized. Even though the Sioux split up into bands and separated after the dance was finished, they were cemented together spiritually and made proudly aware of themselves as members of a great society as a result of their participation in the Sun Dance.

Forbidden to hold the Sun Dance, to wage war, to hunt, and forced to give up their children to teachers who taught them strange ways, a great emptiness came into the lives of the Sioux. Perhaps they could have borne this emptiness quietly and in time have become accustomed to the white man's ways, had it not been for two further developments.

Added to all of the changes the Sioux were forced to accept were the white men's constant attempts to take the Indians' land from them. Since their final surrender to the white men in 1877, the Teton Sioux had given up vast hunting grounds in the Black Hills, the Powder River and Tongue River country, and the Big Horn Basin. They still held by treaty some thirty-five thousand square miles of land.

During the 1870s and 1880s, many attempts were made by the white men to take control of considerable portions of those lands that were still in possession of the Sioux. More than once the Tetons were threatened with wholesale removal to Oklahoma. By 1889 the whites were ready for a final effort to persuade the Indians to give up some of their land. Eastern Dakota had filled with settlers. Railroads had reached the Missouri River and had been forced to stop at the edge of the Great Sioux Reservation. Settlers were demanding that the Indians move aside.

In Washington the Sioux Land Commission was set up. Its chairman was General George Crook, whom the Indians called "The Grey Fox" or "Three Stars." They knew him well. They had fought against him many times. The officials in Washington believed that Crook was just the man to convince the stubborn Indians to accept the government plan to whittle down the Great Sioux Reservation.

General Crook knew the Indians as well as they knew him, and he used every means at his disposal to obtain the required Indian signatures on the land cession agreement.

When Sitting Bull, Red Cloud, and Two Strike advised their people strongly against signing, even though the government promised to pay for the land it took, Crook simply shut these chiefs out of his councils and set up rival chiefs that he could manage. He made extravagant promises to leaders who still had not made up their minds. As a reward for those chiefs who would sign, Crook provided feasts and dances. Overlooking nothing, he even had the ballots in favor of the sale printed in red, those opposed printed in black—knowing that to the Sioux, red symbolized happiness and long life, while black was believed to bring bad luck if improperly used.

Yet even all this was not enough to get the required number of signatures, for it was an old Sioux ruling that three-fourths of all adult males in the Sioux nation had to agree to a disposal of land before a cession was regarded as legal. But this fact did not defeat the Grey Fox. He simply added the necessary signatures. By the end of the summer, it was all over. Nine million acres of their best cattle range had been taken from the Sioux. The Great Sioux Reservation had been whittled down to five small areas that rested like islands inside the Dakota Territory.

There had been great fear among the Indians during the councils with General Crook and the other commissioners that as soon as the government had their land, it would cut their rations, as had happened several times before. Crook assured the Indians that the land agreement had nothing to do with their rations. Some were convinced and signed. Others remained unconvinced. Although Crook had told the truth, the Indian Bureau, on the basis of a new census, reduced the beef issue to the agencies only two weeks after the land agreement had been signed. It was the second such cut in a year. The Sioux were furious. They felt that they had been tricked again.

An old Indian said of the white men: "They made us many promises, more than I can remember, but they kept only one—they promised to take our land and they took it."

That winter the government forbade the Sioux to kill the wild game on their reservation. The Indians considered this restriction an outrage. The slash in their beef rations and another crop failure had brought hunger and in some cases actual starvation to the agencies. There was sickness, too. Epidemics of measles, influenza, and whooping cough carried off children and adults.

The Teton Sioux's cup of bitterness overflowed. Their hopelessness, their flaming hatred for the whites, and their longing to return to the old days left them unusually receptive to the message of the Indian prophet who suddenly appeared.

2

A New World Promised

A STRANGE and wonderful story began to circulate among the Sioux in the summer of 1889. It told of a prophet who had appeared on earth to rescue the Indians from their misery and restore to them their old way of life. With the white men causing them so much hardship, the Indians clutched desperately at this possibility.

In the autumn of that year, the Oglalas on Pine Ridge Agency called a council to discuss the marvelous rumor. Similar councils were held at Rosebud and Cheyenne River. Representatives were selected at all three of the councils to journey westward to seek the source of the story and see whether it was true. The eleven men who were chosen set out together. Good Thunder, Yellow Breast, Flat Iron, Broken Arm, Cloud Horse, Yellow Knife, Elk Horn, and Kicks Back represented Pine Ridge. From Rosebud went Short Bull and Mash-the-Kettle, and from Cheyenne River went Kicking Bear. Short Bull and Kicking Bear were to become the leaders in spreading the new religion among the Sioux.

13

Both men were in their early forties, and both were medicine men. In the old days Kicking Bear had been a mighty warrior and a close friend of Crazy Horse. An Oglala by birth, he became a Miniconjou band chief through marriage to Woodpecker Woman, niece of the Miniconjou chief, Big Foot. Kicking Bear harbored a violent hatred of the white man and all his ways and refused to adjust to the new life.

Short Bull was Kicking Bear's brother-in-law. He, too, had been a great warrior in the old days. A small, sharp-featured man, he was kind and generous to his own people, but a bitter enemy of the whites and of their plans to civilize the Sioux.

The Sioux delegation started west on its quest for the Indian prophet. At most stops along the way, it was joined by emissaries of other tribes who had also heard of the prophet. Their search at last led them to the Paiute Reservation at Walker Lake, Nevada. Here they found the Indian prophet.

He was a Paiute sheepherder named Wovoka. Only a year earlier, he had been an ordinary shaman. But on January 1, 1889, an eclipse of the sun was visible in Nevada. The Paiutes were badly frightened. They wailed and yelled and fired guns into the air in an attempt to drive off the evil monster that threatened to devour the sun, their most powerful god.

Wovoka lay ill with fever in his tepee. At the climax of the sun's eclipse, he seemed to die, but as the shadow slid from the face of the sun, Wovoka returned to life.

I have talked with God [Wakan Tanka] [he told the tribesmen]. Soon now, the earth shall die. But Indians need not be afraid. It is the white men, not the Indians, who should be afraid, for they will be wiped from the face of the earth by a mighty flood of mud and water. When the flood comes, the Indians will be saved. The earth will shake like a dancer's rattle. There will be thunder and smoke and great lightning, for the earth is old and must die. Still, the Indians must not be afraid.

Then, when the flood has passed, the earth will come alive again—just as the sun died and was reborn. The land will be new and green with young grass. Elk and deer and antelope and even the vanished buffalo will return in vast numbers. . . . And all the Indians will be young again and free of the white man's sicknesses—even those of our people who have gone to the grave. It will be a paradise on earth!

Wakan Tanka also explained to Wovoka how the Indians were to prepare for the paradise to come. They were to be honest, good, and work hard. And they were not to fight or to wage war against anyone. They also were supposed to perform a dance that Wakan Tanka taught to Wovoka and to sing special songs. This brand new world—which was to be so much like the old one the Indians had known in happier times—was expected to arrive in the spring of 1891. The ground would tremble as a signal for all Indians to tie sacred eagle feathers in their hair. The feathers would lift them into the sky while the new land covered the old. Then the ghosts of all the Indian dead would rejoin their relatives among the living to people the new earth. Until the new world arrived, Indians could "die" and journey to paradise for a few moments by praying, dancing the Ghost Dance, and singing the Ghost Dance songs.

Wovoka's people, the Paiutes, had become devout followers of the new religion. Gradually word of it had spread to every Indian reservation in the West. The Sioux had come to learn about Wovoka's religion and take it back to their reservation. They remained with Wovoka about a week, listening to his sermons and learning the movements of the Ghost Dance.

The new religion was deeply rooted in Christianity, for Wovoka was well acquainted with the Bible and the religion of the white men. The Ghost Dance religion taught the same values that the white men were trying to teach the Indians in their efforts to civilize them. Above all, it stressed that violence was wrong, even in thought.

Like every other tribe that adopted the new religion, the Sioux changed certain teachings to fit their own psychological needs. Every other tribe accepted Wovoka's nonviolent philosophy. The Sioux did not accept it, however, and their failure to do so was to lead them to tragedy.

The Sioux delegation returned home in March, 1890. They told Wovoka's wonderful story and added a note of their own. Kicking Bear told his people:

> Then Wakan Tanka said to us, "I have neglected you Indians a long time. From now on you shall be under my special care. The earth is getting old and has become rotten in many places. So I will cover the earth with new soil to the depth of five times the height of a man. Under this new land will be buried all the white men; the top of the earth will be covered with sweet grass and running water, and herds of buffalo and wild ponies will stray over it."

Kicking Bear declared that Wakan Tanka had promised to fill up the sea so that no ships could bring other white men to what was rightfully Indian land. Wakan Tanka also promised, said Kicking Bear, to take away from the whites their secret of making gunpowder. Any gunpowder still in the possession of whites—when turned against any Indians who performed the Ghost Dance and practiced the new religion—would be rendered harmless. It was this part of the story that introduced a note of violence into the new religion. If the white men can no longer kill us, the Sioux asked themselves, why shouldn't we defy them and do anything we please? A peaceful religion thus quickly became one of hostility toward the white men.

The story told by Kicking Bear and the other apostles of the new religion spread to every corner of the six Sioux reservations, but not everyone believed it. The young people, who could remember little of the old life and thus did not miss it so much, found Kicking Bear's story hard to swallow. It had a better reception among the older people, however.

The effort to put aside their old ways and take up new ones had caused them much unhappiness, and they looked eagerly to the apostles for instruction in this new religion.

At Rosebud, Short Bull and Mash-the-Kettle began holding councils as soon as they returned from Nevada. Agent J. George Wright knew something was amiss when the Indians began neglecting their farm work. When he learned that the Brules were spending most of their time at the councils Short Bull was holding, Wright called Short Bull into his office and scolded him for luring the people away from their work. The medicine man promised to stop holding the councils.

The apostles at Pine Ridge did not give in so easily. When Agent Hugh D. Gallagher called in Good Thunder and two other Indians to question them about the new religion, they refused to talk. Gallagher locked them in the agency jail, and after two days, although they still refused to answer the agent's questions, they promised to hold no more councils and were released.

At Cheyenne River, Agent McChesney considered the new religion so unimportant that he didn't interfere with Kicking Bear's attempts to convert the Sioux. Kicking Bear sent word to the other agencies summoning all Sioux to a grand council at Cheyenne River to receive instructions in the Ghost Dance. Agents Gallagher and Wright learned of the grand council and warned the Indian leaders on their reservations not to attend. When no one from Rosebud and Pine Ridge came to the council, the excitement over the Ghost Dance died down. About this time, Kicking Bear received a message from the Arapahoes in Wyoming. They had become enthusiastic converts to the new religion, and they wanted a Sioux leader to come at once to Fort Washakie on a matter that they believed to be of the greatest importance to the Indian race.

The Sioux at Standing Rock, Crow Creek, and Lower Brule probably heard of the new religion, but it caused little excitement there. None of the Indians at these agencies had sent delegates to Nevada to see Wovoka, and none of the delegates from the other agencies had yet come to spread the word among them.

Vague rumors of the warlike new religion reached Washington early in June, 1890. Robert V. Belt, acting commissioner of Indian affairs, promptly called for a report from each of the Sioux agents. Gallagher and McChesney admitted that a religious excitement was spreading among the Sioux but declared that they were certain it would die out when the new world failed to appear at the appointed time. At Standing Rock, James McLaughlin, usually the best informed of all the agents about the activities of his people, said he had heard nothing of this new religion.

These agents were correct in discounting the importance of the Ghost Dance movement among the Sioux at that time. Kicking Bear and the other apostles had won over only small numbers of their people to the new faith. Had Congress restored the Indians' rations to their original level, and had it carried out the promises made to the Sioux at the time of the land agreement, the Ghost Dance religion would probably have quietly died out among the Sioux as it did among the other tribes that had accepted Wovoka's teachings.

But Congress did not act, and hunger began to stalk the reservation again. Episcopalian Bishop W. H. Hare, whose church had built more missions and schools on the reservation than any other denomination, estimated that the rations given to the Indians, even when sparingly used, lasted only two-thirds of the period for which they were issued. And when, in mid-July, searing winds whipped across the prairie, withering the crops and gardens, the Indians gave up hope of finally getting enough to eat. In neighboring Nebraska and eastern South Dakota, white settlers abandoned their homesteads and fled back East. The Sioux had to stay. They had no place else to go.

The Brules from the Rosebud Agency went regularly across the Nebraska line to beg at Fort Niobrara, thirty-eight miles away. They knew that the post commissary officer had orders to feed visiting Indians. They also begged for garbage from the company kitchens and for the refuse from the slaughter pens where beef for the soldiers was butchered. Others of the Sioux went to the town of Valentine, Nebraska, to beg.

The bitterness of the Sioux toward their oppressors grew as hunger and sickness carried off more and more of their people. Those chiefs who had fought hardest against the changes forced upon the Indians by the white men stiffened their opposition even more. The agents viewed this hardening of the chiefs' attitudes with alarm.

Of all the chiefs, Sitting Bull had been the most stubborn in his resistance to the white men's program for civilizing the Sioux. He was still the greatest chief and medicine man of the Sioux nation. Surrounded by followers who shared his distaste for the white men's plan, Sitting Bull lived on Standing Rock with his family in a small log cabin forty miles southwest of the agency. Except for the period when he left the reservation to tour as feature attraction with Buffalo Bill's Wild West Show, Sitting Bull had carried on an unceasing feud with Agent McLaughlin. By 1890 he and his sub-chiefs had become so troublesome that McLaughlin suggested they be removed from Standing Rock. Because Sitting Bull and his people had made no specific move to create trouble, however, the Indian Bureau took no action.

At Cheyenne River, the recalcitrants were led by Hump and Big Foot. These two chiefs constantly reminded their people of the old life and urged them to hold out against the white men's efforts to civilize them. Hump, because of his services as scout for Major General Nelson A. Miles, commander of the Division of the Missouri, had earned the job of chief of police at Cheyenne River in spite of his opposition to most of the Indian Bureau's program. Big Foot, after refusing to sign the land agreement, had angrily led his band up the Cheyenne River to a spot eighty miles west of the agency. There they built cabins and sullenly watched white settlers move into the land that had so recently been theirs.

For years those chiefs who would cooperate with the whites had enjoyed considerable influence over their people, strengthened by favors the agents would grant the chiefs and whoever followed them. But now the tide was turning. The hungry summer of 1890 and the prospect of an even hungrier winter to come brought the bitterness of the Sioux to a peak. The chiefs who opposed the whites began to regain some of their power over the people. The Sioux began to hover on the edge of rebellion. Kicking Bear, returning from his visit to the Arapahoes in Wyoming, pushed them over that edge.

3

The Ghost Dances Begin

KICKING BEAR had watched the Arapahoes dance the Ghost Dance and go into trances that enabled them to see friends and relatives who had died long ago. On his way home to his agency in early August, he stopped off for a visit with the Oglalas at Pine Ridge. Kicking Bear's tales of the miracles he had witnessed during his stay among the Arapahoes couldn't have caught the Sioux at a more fertile moment. The Ghost Dance religion promised to relieve the Indians of the despair from which they suffered. If there was a way they could set themselves free of the white men and bring back the old happy life, the Sioux wanted to learn about it.

Red Cloud, aging and almost blind, was still the most prominent chief at Pine Ridge. He played it safe, not wishing to lose the friendship of the agent. Red Cloud expressed doubts about the new religion. If Kicking Bear's story was true, he said, it would spread all over the world. If it was false, it would melt like snow under a hot sun.

The new religion had undergone another alteration. It

was said that an Indian Messiah would come with the arrival of the new world. Unlike Red Cloud, some of the chiefs urged their people to learn the Ghost Dance, reasoning that, should the Messiah appear, the dancers would be in his good graces. Kicking Bear, assisted by Good Thunder, prepared to lead the first Ghost Dance.

A site was picked at the head of Cheyenne Creek. The Oglalas left their cabins and pitched their beloved te-pees in the cottonwood groves along the creek, just as they had done in happier times. The tepees, now made of canvas, formed a circle, and it was within this circle that the Ghost Dance was held. As in the Sun Dance, a small tree was cut and mounted in the center of the circle. After most of its branches were cut off, the tree was painted a sacred red, and colored ribbons were hung from the top. At the base of the tree, Kicking Bear presided over the ceremonies. These began at sunrise. Men and women, who had fasted for twenty-four hours prior to the dance, entered separate sweat lodges for the religious rite of purification. The sweat lodges, shaped like inverted bowls, were made from willows, covered with skins, and floored with a carpet of freshly cut sage. The en-trances of the sweat lodges opened toward the rising sun; facing each entrance from a mound a short distance away was a buffalo skull.

Outside the sweat lodges, medicine men heated stones in a fire and passed them inside by means of forked sticks. The dancers inside the lodges rolled the stones into holes scooped in the floor and poured cold water over them. Clouds of steam filled the small, tightly covered lodges and envel-oped the almost-naked dancers, while the medicine men prayed outside. At last, cleansed of all moral impurities, the dancers emerged and plunged into the nearby creek.

Now Kicking Bear and his assistants prepared the partici-pants for the dance. The dancers' faces were painted with circles, crescents, and crosses that symbolized sun, moon, and morning star. Various colors were used, but red was the sacred color of the Ghost Dance, as it had been of the Sun

Dance. Wovoka had given small cakes of red ochre to the apostles who had come to him in Nevada from the other tribes. Only a few grains of these precious cakes, mixed with the locally made paint of the Sioux, helped a dancer to experience the vision he sought in the Ghost Dance.

As the dancers prepared themselves, each approached the dance pole and tied strips of bright cloth, tiny packages of tobacco, or other offerings suitable for Wakan Tanka to the pole.

By about noon, the dancers were ready. People of all ages and both sexes sat in a large circle facing the center of the dance ring. The leaders stood at the base of the sacred tree. Standing with this group was a young Sioux girl who held an elk-horn bow and four arrows whose bone heads had been dipped in steer's blood. One by one, the girl shot the arrows into the air—one each to the north, south, east, and west. The arrows were then gathered up and tied to the tree, and the girl returned to her position beside it. She remained there throughout the ceremony, holding a sacred redstone pipe toward the west, the direction from which the Messiah and the spirits of those who had died were to appear.

The leader of the dance, after giving detailed directions to his followers, raised his arms to heaven and prayed:

> Great Wakan Tanka, we are ready to begin the dance as you have commanded. Our hearts are now good. We would do all that you ask, and in return for our efforts we beg that you give us back our old hunting grounds and our game. Oh, carry such of the dancers as are really in earnest to the Spirit Land far away and let them there see their dead relatives. Show them what good things you have prepared for us and return the visitors safely to earth again. Hear us, we pray.

Following this chant, the leader passed around a vessel filled with sacred meat—beef that had been blessed and symbolized the flesh of the vanished buffalo that would soon return in vast herds to darken the plains. When all the dancers had eaten a bit of the meat, they stood and joined hands. The leader began a song. It was slow and rhythmic. The others joined in.

> The father says so—E' yayo!
> The father says so—E' yayo!
> The father says so,
> The father says so.
> You shall see your grandfather—E' yayo!
> You shall see your grandfather—E' yayo!
> The father says so,
> The father says so.
> You shall see your kindred—E' yayo!
> You shall see your kindred—E' yayo!
> The father says so,
> The father says so!

The voices became shrill and filled with emotion. The dancers' bodies began to bob slowly up and down, and with a shuffling side step they began to move the dance ring toward the left. The movement was slow and the effect hypnotic.

> Someone comes to tell news, to tell news.
> There shall be a buffalo chase,
> There shall be a buffalo chase.
> Make arrows, make arrows.

After half an hour, the singing and dancing stopped. "Weep for your sins!" the leader cried. Moans and wails rose from the dance ring. Some dancers rolled on the ground, crying for forgiveness. Others rushed to the prayer tree and thrust gifts among its limbs. A few of the dancers slashed themselves with knives and smeared their blood on the tree in the ancient way of showing grief.

At a signal from the leader, the dance began again. The dancers moved faster now, exalting and singing of the world to come.

> The people are coming home,
> The people are coming home,
> Saith my father, saith my father,
> Saith my father.
> The time cometh, I shall see him,
> The time cometh, I shall see him,
> Saith my mother, saith my mother.

Faster went the dancers, bending and weaving. Other songs spontaneously burst forth. The dancers' arms and legs twitched and their bodies trembled. They leaped wildly forward, backward, and into the air. Singing gave way to wailing and shouting. The leaders dashed around the circle, urging the dancers to yet higher pitches of delirium. Many of the dancers collapsed and lay rigid in trances. It was in these trances that some of the dancers beheld the visions they had sought. When they revived a few minutes later, the visionaries told of seeing dead relatives in the Spirit Land.

Black Elk, a young Oglala shaman who, as a boy, had experienced a great vision that showed him how he might save his people, was present at this first dance, although he did not participate. Black Elk had gone only to see and to learn what the people believed. On the second day, he decided to join the dancers.

> So I dressed myself in a sacred manner, [he said] and before the dance began the next morning I went among the people who were standing around the withered tree. Good Thunder, who was a relative of my father and later married my mother, put his arms around me and took me to the sacred tree that had not bloomed, and there he offered up a prayer for me. He said: "Father, Great Spirit, behold this boy! Your ways he shall see!" Then he began to cry.
>
> I thought of my father and my brother and sister who had died, and I could not keep the tears from running out of my eyes. I raised my face to keep them back, but they came out just the same. I cried with my whole heart, and while I cried

I thought of my people in despair. I thought of my vision, and how it was promised me that my people should have a place in this earth where they could be happy every day. I thought of them on the wrong road now, but maybe they could be brought back into the hoop [sacred circle] again and to the good road.

Under the tree that never bloomed I stood and cried because it had withered away. With tears on my face I asked the Great Spirit to give it life and leaves and singing birds, as in my vision.

Then there came a strong shivering all over my body, and I knew that the power was in me.

Good Thunder now took one of my arms, Kicking Bear the other, and we began to dance. The song we sang was like this:

>   Who do you think he is that comes?
>   It is one who seeks his mother!

It was what the dead would sing when entering the other world and looking for their relatives who had gone there before them.

As I danced, with Good Thunder and Kicking Bear holding my arms between them, I had the queer feeling that had come to me before and I seemed to be lifted clear off the ground. I did not have a vision all that first day. That night I thought about the other world and that the Wanekia [Wovoka] himself was with my people there and maybe the holy tree of my vision was really blooming yonder right then, and that it was there my vision had already come true. From the center of the earth I had been shown all good and beautiful things in a great circle of peace, and maybe this land of my vision was where all my people were going, and there they would live and prosper where no white men were or could ever be.

Before we started dancing next day, Kicking Bear offered a prayer, saying: "Father, Great Spirit, behold these people! They shall go forth today to see their relatives, and yonder they shall be happy, day after day, and their happiness will not end."

Then we began dancing, and most of the people wailed and cried as they danced, holding hands in a circle; but some of them laughed with happiness. Now and then someone would fall down like dead, and others would go staggering around and panting before they would fall. While they were lying there like dead, they were having visions, and we kept on dancing and singing, and many were crying for the old way of living and that the old religion might be with them again.

After awhile I began to feel very queer. First, my legs seemed to be full of ants. I was dancing with my eyes closed, as the others did. Suddenly it seemed that I was swinging off the ground and not touching it any longer. The queer feeling came up from my legs and was in my heart now. It seemed I would glide forward like a swing, and then glide back again in longer and longer swoops. There was no fear in this, just a growing happiness.

I must have fallen down, but I felt as though I had fallen off a swing when it was going forward, and I was floating head first through the air. My arms were stretched out, and all I saw at first was a single eagle feather right in front of me. Then the feather was a spotted eagle dancing on ahead of me with his wings fluttering, and he was making the shrill whistle that is his. My body did not move at all, but I looked ahead and floated fast toward where I looked.

There was a ridge in front of me, and I thought I was going to run into it, but I went right over it. On the other side of the ridge I could see a beautiful land where many, many people were camping in a great circle. I could see that they were happy and had plenty. Everywhere there were drying racks full of meat. The air was clear and beautiful with a living light that was everywhere. All around the circle, feeding on the green, green grass, were fat and happy horses; and animals of all kinds were scattered all over the green hills, and singing hunters were returning with their meat.

I floated over the tepees and began to come down feet first at the center of the hoop where I could see a beautiful tree all green and full of flowers. When I touched the ground, two men were coming toward me, and they wore holy shirts made and painted in a certain way. They came to me and said: "It is not yet time to see your father, who is happy. You have work to do. We will give you something that you shall carry back to your people, and with it they shall come to see their loved ones."

I knew it was the way their holy shirts were made that they wanted me to take back. They told me to return at once, and then I was out in the air again, floating fast as before. When I came right over the dancing place, the people were still dancing, but

it seemed they were not making any sound. I had hoped to see
the withered tree in bloom, but it was dead.

Then I fell back into my body, and as I did this I heard voices
all around and above me, and I was sitting on the ground. Many
were crowding around, asking me what vision I had seen. I
told them just what I had seen, and what I brought back was
the memory of the holy shirts the two men wore.[1]

Black Elk made several of the Ghost Shirts, and from that
time on every dancer wore one. Worn above buckskin leggings, the Ghost Shirt was a loose garment made of cotton
cloth or muslin, and ornamented, like the faces of the dancers,
with painted circles, crescents, and crosses, and with designs
symbolizing the eagle, magpie, crow, and other birds and animals of special significance to the Sioux. The most popular
design was that of a young eagle with outstretched wings
painted in blue on the back of the shirts. Many of the garments
were fringed and adorned with feathers.

The women dancers wore loose dresses made and decorated in the same way as the shirts. For the first time, women
were permitted to wear eagle plumes in their hair. This
made them feel a new sense of importance.

The belief grew among the Sioux that the Ghost Shirts and
Ghost Dresses would be bulletproof. After all, hadn't Kicking
Bear told them that Wakan Tanka would render the gunpowder of the whites harmless when turned against any Indians who performed the Ghost Dance? The medicine men
declared that if soldiers fired at an Indian who was wearing
one of the sacred garments, their bullets would fall harmlessly to the ground. This was not a new idea. Sioux warriors
had long worn "medicine shirts" designed to turn away the
bullets and arrows of an enemy. The Sioux drew courage
from the belief that the white soldiers were no longer to be
dreaded.

[1] John Neihardt, *Black Elk Speaks* (Lincoln, Nebraska: University of Nebraska Press, 1961), pp. 243-247.

Wovoka had decreed that, because the world to come would bear no trace of the white man, nothing of white manufacture could be used in the Ghost Dance. This meant that a dancer could wear no jewelry or belts made of white men's materials. Nor could the dancers carry metal knives or guns. At first the Sioux heeded this rule, but as time passed and the dance became increasingly warlike, a rifle or two would be brought into the dance circle.

The first Ghost Dance camp broke up after the fifth day of dancing. Kicking Bear went from there to Chief Hump's camp near the mouth of Cherry Creek to teach the dance to the people there. Kicking Bear was met at Cherry Creek by his wife, Woodpecker Woman, and her uncle, Big Foot. Short Bull and Mash-the-Kettle went to the nearby Rosebud Agency to spread the new religion.

Within two weeks of the first Ghost Dance, the Oglalas on Pine Ridge had reached a pitch of feverish enthusiasm. At first the dances were held only on Sunday, "the great medicine day of the white men." Later, as the faithful began to count more and more on their ability to bring forth the paradise that had been foreseen by Wovoka, they staged the dances more frequently and abandoned their cabins and corn fields to live permanently in tepees at the dance camps.

Hugh Gallagher, the head of the Pine Ridge Agency, became alarmed. Also alarmed were the white farmers who had settled near the reservation. Most whites harbored the fear that the Indians would someday take to the warpath again. The settlers demanded that Gallagher use his Indian police to stop the dances by force. On August 22 Gallagher sent a squad of the police to Torn Belly's camp on White Clay Creek, eighteen miles north of the agency, with instructions to break up the dance and send the people home. The police returned the following morning and informed Agent Gallagher that they had been ignored and that the Indians were preparing to dance the following day, Sunday, August 24.

Gallagher decided to take a first-hand look at the ceremony. On Sunday morning, he rode to the dance grounds himself, taking with him twenty policemen and two other men—Philip Wells, an interpreter and scout, and Special Agent E. B. Reynolds. They found 150 tepees scattered around the cabins of Torn Belly's band. A dance ground lay in the center of the camp. Within it stood a prayer tree from which flew an American flag. There wasn't a living soul in sight. The Indians had found out the agent was coming, had called off the dance, and had hidden themselves in a grove of trees along the bank of White Clay Creek.

Gallagher halted his party in the center of the dance circle. At this moment two Indians emerged from their hiding places, dropped to their knees, and pointed the muzzles of their rifles at the intruders. Angry at being threatened, Gallagher ordered his police to arrest the two. Interpreter Wells translated the order but immediately countermanded it on his own responsibility. He was convinced that the agent was asking for more trouble than he could handle. It was obvious from the number of lodges that some six hundred dancers were gathered there.

When the police failed to move forward, Gallagher spurred his horse and rode toward the two challenging Indians. Wells, whom the Indians liked and trusted, pushed in front of Gallagher to protect him. Suddenly the heads of several other Indians popped above the creek bank.

Gallagher stopped. "What do you mean, drawing your guns on me, your agent?" he demanded.

Wells translated and added, on his own, to one of the Indians who was the father of a good friend of his: "Father, I want you to obey me. Put down that gun."

The Indian replied, "Yes, my son, I will obey you," and he laid his rifle on the ground. To Gallagher he said, "If you have come to talk to me in peace, why bring so many guns?"

While the agent groped for an explanation, more Indians sprang into view with rifles at the ready. The police swiftly drew their revolvers, and for one tense moment the two groups teetered on the edge of battle.

At this critical moment, Young-Man-Afraid-of-His-Horses rode into the dance circle. Respected by whites and Indians alike, his very presence calmed both sides. Wells quickly explained to him that the agent had come merely to watch the dance, not to stop it. The warriors, reassured, lowered their rifles.

Torn Belly came out of the grove of trees and invited the visitors to stay and watch the Ghost Dance. The remainder of the Indians then emerged from the trees and began the ceremony.

The dance shocked Gallagher and Reynolds. Reynolds informed Washington that it should be forbidden, and he added an ominous warning. Reynolds did not think the Ghost Dance could be stopped except by sending in the army.

Gallagher, too, warned his superiors that the dance should be stopped, but he had no intention of getting mixed up in a potentially very dangerous situation. He had lately received word that he was being replaced. A Republican president had been elected, and a Republican was being appointed as agent of Pine Ridge. While Gallagher sat back and awaited his successor, the Ghost Dance craze spread through the Oglalas at Pine Ridge and, with the force and heat of a prairie fire, swept into the neighboring Rosebud Reservation.

4

The Sioux Grow Militant

THE TENSION increased sharply in September, 1890. It was in that month that the Ghost Dance craze seized the Sioux on the Rosebud, where Short Bull taught the Brules the dance. Drawn irresistibly to the new religion, the Indians abandoned their fields and cabins and withdrew their children from the schools to travel to the dance camps.

By the middle of the month, when the Brules flocked to the agency to collect their biweekly rations, they could talk of nothing but the new religion. Those who had performed the Ghost Dance exchanged stories about their trips to the Spirit Land. The excitement and hope inspired by the dance were contagious.

Into this emotion-charged atmosphere came a rumor that soldiers had arrived at Fort Niobrara, a few miles away, and were coming to stop the Ghost Dances and punish the dancers. Indian men rushed to their lodges, stripped to breechcloths, and painted themselves in the sacred manner for war. Then, snatching up their weapons and leaping on their ponies, they headed southward toward the fort. When Agent Wright discovered what had happened, he rode out in pursuit and found the warriors drawn up across the road to Fort Niobrara, waiting for the troops. With much difficulty, Wright finally persuaded the Indians that the rumor was false and that they should return to the agency.

The incident angered Wright. He decided that the time had come to assert his authority. He called an assembly of Indians the next day and ordered them to stop the Ghost Dance. Until they obeyed, he would issue no more rations, Wright declared.

This action had a sobering effect upon the Brules. They packed up and went home, and before long their empty stomachs dampened the enthusiasm most of them had felt for the dance. When Agent Wright was satisfied that most of his Indians had given up the dance, he began issuing rations once more. Only a small corps of fanatics refused to abandon a religion that they believed would free them to live as they were meant to live.

No sooner had Wright brought the situation under control than he found himself in trouble from another quarter. A government inspector arrived at the agency to investigate the sharp drop in population recorded by the recent census. The new count of Indians on the Rosebud Reservation was 5,250, yet Wright had been receiving rations for 7,500. After a quick look at the evidence, the inspector accused Wright of selling the extra rations and putting the money in his own pocket. The inspector immediately suspended Wright. The charge against the agent was untrue, and although Wright managed to prove his innocence and was back on the job by December, it was too late.

Special Agent E. B. Reynolds, who had been visiting the Pine Ridge Agency, was appointed to take Wright's place temporarily. Reynolds knew little about the situation on Rosebud and nothing about the personalities of the Indian leaders with whom he would have to deal. Spurred on by Short Bull, the Brules immediately seized on this advantage and resumed the Ghost Dance. Their attitude grew more militant. The Indians wanted arms and ammunition, and to get money they sold their ponies and other possessions. Many Brules had been making a little money by cutting and delivering firewood to the agency. These Indians went to the trading posts to cash the receipts they had been given in payment for their work, accepting as little as one-third of the face value of the receipts. Tired of being half hungry most of the time, the Indians began to slaughter cattle that the government had given them for breeding stock to build their own herds.

Reynolds set out to put a stop to this situation. He sent some members of the Indian police force to arrest several of the men known to be butchering the cattle. When the police tried to arrest the men, seventy-five armed warriors moved forward, and the police withdrew.

Later, when Reynolds himself spoke to some of the Indians to protest the killing of the cattle, he was told that they would rather die fighting than from starvation. Besides, they said, they had no reason to fear death. When the new world that Wovoka promised arrived, all dead Indians would be brought back to life.

Trouble was brewing on the Cheyenne River Reservation, too. Agent Charles McChesney, capable and knowledgeable about the Indians, had been replaced. Under the spoils system, agency appointments had been put entirely into the hands of senators and representatives. The congressmen chose men for these sensitive jobs for no better reason than that they were friends or party supporters. It was a rare man who took to his job as agent any special knowledge or understanding of Indians. Typical of the type of man who received an agency appointment was Perain P. Palmer, who was selected by South Dakota Congressman J. A. Pickler to replace Agent McChesney.

Congressman Pickler assured the secretary of the interior that Palmer was "a cool man and a man of good judgement." Whether this was Pickler's honest evaluation of the man or whether it was a casual disregard for the truth, Palmer did not live up to the congressman's evaluation of him.

Inexperienced, arriving at the agency at a time when emotions among the Indians were running high, Palmer encountered trouble right at the start. His first move was to inform the dancers that the Department of the Interior was displeased with their behavior. In a report to the Indian commissioner of this first confrontation, Palmer said he received the reply that "the Indians are displeased with the Department *and will dance.*"

The Miniconjous on Cheyenne River had by this time been converted to the Ghost Dance by Kicking Bear, who, after bringing the incendiary new religion to Pine Ridge and Rosebud, had returned to his own reservation. Exhibiting from the first more than the usual resistance to the changes the whites were forcing upon them, the Miniconjous embraced the new religion with revolutionary zeal. Sioux from the other reservations flocked to Cheyenne River to confer with Kicking Bear and learn all they could about the dance and the promises Wovoka had made. They sought inspiration from the fiery apostle who had seen and talked with the prophet himself. Hump, a powerful chief who had cooperated with the whites to the extent of becoming chief of the agency police, exchanged his police uniform for a Ghost Shirt and began to hold dances. Soon his camp was swollen by four hundred Miniconjous who had come to dance.

On the banks of the Cheyenne River, the same wild scenes could be observed in Big Foot's camp. His small band, too, soon grew with new arrivals who had come to take part in the frenzied ceremonies. Indians in Big Foot's village danced day and night, freed at last from their hopelessness and pouring their energy into an activity they believed would bring back their old way of life.

After meeting defiance in his first attempt to stop the dancers, Agent Palmer tried again. He sent Straight Head, who had been appointed to replace Hump as chief of police, with some men to the camps of Hump and Big Foot. The policemen, met by dancers armed with Win-

chester rifles, retreated. Several similar attempts to stop the
dances met with the same failure.

All sorts of wild rumors began to sweep through the
Dakotas and Nebraska, spreading alarm among the settlers
there. The agents were reported to have lost control, and
the Indians were thought to be getting ready to raid the
ranches and settlements. Another rumor said the Indians
had already broken out of the reservations and were fanning out to burn and kill. Thoroughly frightened, the settlers met at Rushville and Valentine in Nebraska and
Pierre and Bismarck in the Dakotas to draft resolutions
calling upon the government for help. The settlers wanted
troops sent to the reservations, and they wanted arms and
ammunition for themselves. Many of them abandoned their
homesteads and took refuge in the towns and villages that
bordered the reservations. Some of the whites, ruined by
the same drought that had withered the Indians' cornfields
and gardens, gave the wild land a parting curse and went
back East.

The Standing Rock Reservation, home of Sitting Bull, was
the northernmost Sioux agency. It stretched across what
is now the line between the two Dakotas. Kicking Bear's
Cheyenne River Reservation was immediately to the south.
Eager to learn more of the religious fervor that was sweeping
the other reservations, Sitting Bull began to plead with
Agent McLaughlin for a pass to visit Cheyenne River.

McLaughlin and Sitting Bull had been antagonists from
the day Sitting Bull had been placed on the Standing Rock
Reservation. The chief had resisted surrender to the white
man more stubbornly than any other Sioux leader with the
exception of Crazy Horse. Sitting Bull had fled with his
band into Canada rather than submit to being penned up
on a reservation. But life had been hard in Canada, too,
and at last Sitting Bull had accepted the inevitable and
had surrendered.

McLaughlin's orders were the same as those issued to the

other agents—break the authority of the chiefs. McLaughlin had tried numerous means, but Sitting Bull could not be broken. His courage, honesty, and wisdom were exceptional. Sitting Bull was a natural aristocrat, and he attracted respect and admiration as a magnet attracts iron. His honesty extended even to his personal enemies—including McLaughlin. Sitting Bull thought McLaughlin was a good agent and said so. McLaughlin, on the other hand, never once, in all the reports he filed in Washington, had a good word to say about Sitting Bull. McLaughlin was an immigrant, a young man of limited education, driven by unbounded ambition, jealous and resentful of all rivals to his power. The fact that Sitting Bull retained his authority over his people in spite of all McLaughlin's efforts was impossible for the agent to accept. He never gave up his attempts to break Sitting Bull. Now he turned down Sitting Bull's repeated requests for a pass to visit the Cheyenne River Reservation.

Knowing that McLaughlin had spies watching his every move, Sitting Bull realized he could not simply slip away. Therefore he sent an invitation to Kicking Bear to come north and reveal the mysteries of the new religion to his people. At the meeting on Grand River, Kicking Bear told Sitting Bull's band of his meeting with Wovoka and of the miracles the prophet had declared would come to pass if only the Indians would dance a special dance. Sitting Bull's people—starving, despairing, grieving deeply over the loss of their old, beloved way of life—grasped eagerly at the promise that their old life would be restored to them. They begged Kicking Bear to teach them the Ghost Dance immediately.

Sitting Bull, however, could not believe such a story. "It is impossible for a dead man to return and live again," he said.

Sitting Bull also argued that the soldiers would come and stop this dance as they had stopped the Sun Dance; but

Kicking Bear said he need not worry. Even if the soldiers came, they could not harm the people, for the Ghost Shirts the dancers wore could not be pierced by bullets.

This assertion did not seem improbable to Sitting Bull. He had known several men who seemed impervious to bullets. After giving the matter some thought, he declared that if his people wanted the Ghost Dance, then they would have it. Sitting Bull erected a prayer tree and set up a large tent from which to superintend the dances.

At first Sitting Bull danced with the others, hoping to "die" and be able to talk once again with his daughter, who had recently died. But a trance would not come. He listened eagerly to more successful dancers who had talked with relatives long dead.

It was about this time that Philip Wells, the interpreter at Pine Ridge, wrote a letter to Agent McLaughlin at Standing Rock warning him to prevent the dance from being introduced there if he could. "I say this because you or anyone else can have no idea how . . . it takes hold of the Indians as some of our best Indians are nearly crazy over it," Wells wrote.

Once McLaughlin learned that Kicking Bear was on the reservation, he sent a dozen police to order the chief back to his own agency. Crazy Walking, the captain who commanded the small detachment of police, was so awed by the spectacle of the Ghost Dance that he could not summon the courage to carry out his orders. He simply told Sitting Bull that Kicking Bear must leave. Then Crazy Walking himself left, taking his men back to the agency. Sitting Bull stopped dancing at once, but he failed to stop the others. Courtesy would not permit him to drive Kicking Bear and his assistants away, nor would pride allow Sitting Bull to leave his home and divorce himself from the dancers. It would look as if he had been run out of his own camp.

McLaughlin, disgusted with Crazy Walking, assigned the mission to Lieutenant Chatka, who set out with only two men. Seemingly immune to the bewitchment of the dance and unawed by Kicking Bear, he marched through a ring of dancers and confronted the apostle. Chatka commanded that Kicking Bear obey the agent's orders at once and escorted him and his six companions to the reservation boundary.

But it was too late. Kicking Bear had infected the Standing Rock Sioux with the same fanatical faith that had spread among the other reservations. As Sitting Bull's dances along the Grand River grew wilder, settlers there, too, began to worry. Newspapers in the nearby towns of Bismarck and Mandan carried stories about the increasing militancy of the Indians and began asking that some action be taken to prevent a possible uprising.

On October 17 Agent McLaughlin wrote a letter to the commissioner of Indian affairs and reported the progress that the Ghost Dance had made on Standing Rock in only a month. McLaughlin did not think the situation was out of control, but to quiet the Indians and insure that the dance craze would burn itself out, he suggested that Sitting Bull be removed from the reservation and held in a military prison until such time as it seemed wise to allow him to return to Standing Rock.

When the letter arrived in Washington, Commissioner Thomas J. Morgan was in Oklahoma visiting Indian schools. It was Acting Commissioner Robert V. Belt who received the letter. Belt approved of McLaughlin's recommendation, but he realized that the arrest of Sitting Bull would be sharply attacked by critics of the government's Indian program. Belt wanted the criticism to fall elsewhere than on the Indian Bureau and the Department of the Interior. He therefore suggested to Secretary of the Interior John W. Noble that the secretary of war be asked to have the army arrest Sitting Bull, as well as the other chiefs.

But Secretary Noble would not agree to such drastic action when, as far as he could see, the situation did not warrant it. Commissioner Belt relayed the secretary's refusal and made some suggestions of his own. McLaughlin, he said, must tell

Sitting Bull and the other chiefs that Secretary Noble was "greatly displeased with their conduct" and would hold Sitting Bull to a "strict personal responsibility for the misconduct, acts of violence, or any threats, actions, or movements" that might result from his influence. In other words, if any trouble erupted, Sitting Bull himself would be punished. Sitting Bull was to be told that he must submit to government authority immediately and direct his people "to turn their backs upon the medicine men who are seeking to divert the Indians from the ways of civilization."

McLaughlin understood Indians better than Belt and knew that Sitting Bull would probably secretly laugh at any man who thought he could intimidate the chief with such a feeble threat. The message was never passed on to Sitting Bull.

Although the Indian Bureau had refused McLaughlin's request to have Sitting Bull arrested, the agent did not give up the idea. He was convinced that eventually it would be necessary to remove the great chief from the reservation, for his authority over his people appeared to be complete and unquestioned. One day McLaughlin called a meeting of the Indian policemen and informed them that it might be necessary to arrest Sitting Bull. The announcement startled the police. Some believed it would be impossible to arrest Sitting Bull. Others thought there was no need for such drastic action. All agreed that the arrest could not be made without bloodshed. Sitting Bull's followers would not stand idly by and watch their chief being carted off to prison. Many of the police had relatives in Sitting Bull's camp who might be killed during the battle that was certain to erupt. The policemen also demanded to know who would care for their own widows and orphans if they were killed while trying to arrest Sitting Bull.

Frightened and refusing to take part in the plan, Crazy Walking, captain of the police, Grasping Eagle, Big Mane, and Standing Soldier resigned. One Bull, nephew of Sitting Bull, was discharged. McLaughlin knew that One Bull loved his uncle and could not be counted on to help with the arrest.

The agent then enlisted new policemen from Sitting Bull's own camp, but when they learned what McLaughlin wanted them to do, they turned in their badges and uniforms. They did not wish to kill their own people, and they refused to become *ceska maza*—"metal breasts." The Sioux had given the Indian police this name because of the metal badges they wore.

It was Lieutenant Bull Head who solved Agent McLaughlin's problem. Bull Head lived three miles west of Sitting Bull's camp on the south side of Grand River. For a long time there had been bad blood between the lieutenant and the chief. The enmity had resulted from a quarrel between Catch-the-Bear, Sitting Bull's assistant, and Bull Head, in which Sitting Bull had publicly sided with Catch-the-Bear. Bull Head's humiliation had not faded, and he welcomed the chance for revenge. "Let me pick my own men," he told the agent. "I can find men who will do the job."

Bull Head found his men on Sitting Bull's reservation. They were brave men, men such as Iron Thunder, Good-Voiced Eagle, Running Hawk, Black Pheasant, White Bird, Weasel Bear, and One Feather. At a special meeting, McLaughlin promised government pensions to them and their families if they were killed or wounded should Sitting Bull's followers put up a fight.

After the meeting, Sergeant Shave Head reeled into the home of some of his relatives, emotionally shaken. "Do not be ashamed," he hastened to reassure them. "I am not drunk. I only seem that way. I am a dead man. I am here in spirit, but my body is lying on the prairie. We have been ordered to arrest Sitting Bull." His relatives began to cry.

Sitting Bull exploded with indignation when he learned that McLaughlin planned to arrest him. "Why does he keep trying to humble me?" he asked.

Can I be any lower than I am? Once I was a man, but now I am a pitiful wretch—no country, no fast horses, no guns worth having. I was rich, now I am poor. What more does he want

to do to me? I was a fool ever to come down here. I should
have stayed with the Red Coats in the Grandmother's country
[Canada].

From that day on, Sitting Bull believed his days to be
numbered. He no longer went to the agency but asked others
to collect his rations for him there on ration day.

The situation was worse at Pine Ridge. On October 9
Agent Gallagher's replacement arrived. He was Daniel F.
Royer, a man who had tried his hand at many professions
and apparently had succeeded at none. He had been a physi-
cian, druggist, newspaperman, banker, and member of the
South Dakota legislature for two terms. He had no qualifi-
cations for his new job, and why he accepted it is a mystery.
He knew nothing about Indians—in fact, they frightened
him—but the job was a political plum, and it was presented
to Royer by Senator Richard F. Pettigrew of his home state.
Perhaps Royer was too timid to refuse.

The Indians took their measure of Royer immediately and
nicknamed him "Young-Man-Afraid-of-Indians." Gallagher,
knowing he was to be replaced by a Republican appointee,
had allowed matters at Pine Ridge to drift, and by the time
Royer came on the job, the Indians were nearly out of hand.
Interpreter Philip Wells wrote to McLaughlin at Standing
Rock that Royer "has got an elephant on his hands as the
craze had taken such a hold on the Indians before he took
charge."

Royer's position was not helped by the message he found
on his desk when he arrived at the agency. It was from Acting
Commissioner Belt, who instructed him to "warn the Indians
that said 'ghost dance' will not be allowed on any occasion."
Unlike McLaughlin, who refused to pass along such a message to Sitting Bull, Royer relayed the message. Accompanied
by some Indian police, he visited the dance camp and ordered
the ceremony stopped. One Indian stepped forward and said,
"White people dance when they wish to. So do the Sioux."

And the ceremony continued. Royer returned to the agency, not knowing what to do next. After only four days on the job, he wrote Commissioner Belt that he thought the army might have to be called in.

Belt replied: "I approve of your course in using persuasion with the chiefs and think you had better continue in that direction."

The Oglalas turned a deaf ear to Royer's attempts at persuasion and grew more and more fanatical in their allegiance to the new religion. They withdrew their children from the whites' schools, slaughtered breeding stock, and contemptuously defied the agent and his police at every turn. Some of the chiefs who had been cooperating with the government in its attempts to convert their brothers to a new way of life backed Royer and tried to persuade the dancers to break up the dance camps, go back to their cabins, and tend their fields. But in this case the government had done its work too well. It had set out to break the power of the chiefs and had succeeded. The Oglalas gave no more heed to the chiefs who supported Royer than they did to the agent. Red Cloud, who had managed to cooperate to some extent with the government and still retain much of the power he held over his people, said nothing. The dancers suspected that the chief, old and nearly blind, stood with them in this matter.

Less than a week after Belt's letter advocating more persuasion reached Royer, Major General Nelson A. Miles visited Pine Ridge. He was chairman of a commission that had been sent to investigate certain complaints of the Northern Cheyennes. Miles had earned a reputation as an Indian fighter and had been appointed commanding general of the Division of the Missouri, which included the reservations in the Dakotas and Nebraska.

When Miles arrived at Pine Ridge, Agent Royer told him of his anxiety over the situation on the reservation. The general, after hearing the story, seemed convinced that the dance craze would die out in time. To hasten its demise, he called a council of the Oglala chiefs the next day and gave them a fatherly lecture. This technique often had worked in the past. It did not work now.

Chief Little Wound rose to speak and declared that he wanted his people to stop acting like white men. They were Indians and should live like Indians. The Ghost Dance would allow them to do so by bringing back their old free life. Little Wound asked General Miles to write his words down, show the paper to the Great Father in Washington, and tell him that Little Wound and his people would dance as long as they pleased.

Not for years had the Sioux shown such defiance to an army officer, especially one as important as General Miles. When he left the next day, Miles must have carried with him an impression of the situation that was entirely different from the one he had formed after his first talk with Royer.

After the Miles commission left, Royer made one more attempt to persuade the Indians to stop the Ghost Dance. When the chiefs laughed at him and repeated that it was their intention to dance as long as they pleased, Royer fired off a letter to Belt. In one long, unpunctuated sentence, Royer revealed all the fear, helplessness, and frustration he was experiencing.

> Your dept. has been informed of the damage resulting from these dances and of the danger attending them of the crazy Indians doing serious damage to others and the different Agencies I suppose report about the same but I have carefully studied the matter for almost 6 wks [sic] and have brot all the persuasion to bear on the leaders that was possible but without effect and the only remedy for this matter is the use of military and until this is done you need not expect any progress from these people on the other hand you will be made to realize that they are tearing down more in a day than the Government can build in a month.

Only one day after Royer mailed this letter, the situation became more menacing. Near the boundary between the Pine

Ridge and Rosebud reservations, Short Bull, the Brule apostle, made a spectacular announcement to a huge crowd of believers who had assembled to hear him.

My friends and relations: I will soon start this thing in running order. I have told you that this would come to pass in two seasons, but since the whites are interfering so much, I will advance the time from what my father above told me to do, so the time will be shorter. Therefore you must not be afraid of anything . . .

Now, there will be a tree sprout up, and there all the members of our religion and the tribe must gather together. That will be the place where we will see our dead relations. But before this time we must dance the balance of this moon [November], at the end of which time the earth will shiver very hard. Whenever this thing occurs, I will start the wind to blow. We are the ones who will then see our fathers, mothers, and everybody. We, the tribe of Indians, are the ones who are living a sacred life. God, our father himself, has told and commanded and shown me to do these things.

Short Bull added a warning. The Indians must not permit the white man to interfere with this last, great dance.

"There may be soldiers around you," he said,

but pay no attention to them, continue to dance. If the soldiers surround you four deep, three of you on whom I have put holy shirts will sing a song, which I have taught you, around them, when some of them will drop dead, then the rest will start to run, but their horses will sink into the earth; the riders will jump from their horses, but they will sink into the earth also; then you can do as you desire with them. Now you must know this, that all the soldiers and that race will be dead; there will be only five thousand left living on the earth. My friends and relations, this is straight and true.

Now, we must gather at Pass Creek where the tree is sprouting. There we will go among our dead relations. You must not take any earthly things with you. Then the men must take off all their clothing and the women must do the same. No one shall be ashamed of exposing their persons. My father above has told us to do this, and we must do as he says. You must not be afraid of anything. The guns are the only things we are afraid of, but they belong to our father in heaven. He will see that they do no harm. Whatever white men may tell you, do not listen to them, my relations. This is all.

With the promise of the arrival of paradise in only one moon's time, Oglalas from Pine Ridge and Brules from Rosebud flocked to Short Bull's camp. Kicking Bear arrived to lend his authority to the proceedings. To the north, on Standing Rock, Sitting Bull kept himself informed of the happenings on Pass Creek. Runners from the dance site kept arriving to urge Sitting Bull to join the group.

Perhaps it was at this point that the Ghost Dance took an irreversible direction. As first promulgated, it was a religion that advocated peace and nonviolence as a means of bringing back to the Indians their old way of life. Even Short Bull's message admonishing the Ghost Dancers not to permit soldiers to interfere with this last great dance was a defensive move, nonviolent in nature. The dancers were to attack only if soldiers tried to stop them, and their only weapon was to be a special song.

But many of Short Bull's followers lost sight of the fact that they were to act only in defense of the dance. In their minds the whole affair began to take on the character of a holy war against the white man. Army reports began to arrive in Washington stating that messengers were being sent by Sitting Bull to tribes as far north as Canada, urging them to meet in the spring at Bear Butte, near the Black Hills, for the purpose of driving all white men from the country. No concrete proof exists that Sitting Bull, Short Bull, or Kicking Bear sent such messages, or if they did, that the content was anything other than the typical campaign rhetoric of leaders everywhere.

By this time the pressure on the White House from settlers, agents, and the newspapers to take some action was too great to be ignored. President Harrison, on October 31, directed the secretary of war to order an investigation into conditions in the Sioux country. Because General Miles had not yet returned from his investigation of the Cheyenne problem, Brigadier General Thomas H. Ruger, commanding the Department of Dakota, was sent to the Standing Rock and Cheyenne River reservations to investigate.

At Standing Rock, Ruger decided that Agent McLaughlin had his people under control, and that, with the help of Lieutenant Colonel William F. Drum from nearby Fort Yates, he could handle any trouble that should arise.

On Cheyenne River, the situation was not so encouraging but still not threatening. Ruger ordered up a company of infantry from Fort Sully to reinforce the company already quartered at Fort Bennett, the reservation's military post.

By early November, Agent Reynolds, who was still filling in for Wright at Rosebud while Wright was trying to prove himself innocent of the charge that he had been selling Indian rations, had found himself no match for Short Bull and the fanatical fervor he had excited among the Brules for the Ghost Dance. Reynolds's efforts to stop the Ghost Dance and regain control over the Indians had failed. He reported to Washington that "there appears to be but one remedy . . . and that is a sufficient force of troops to prevent an outbreak, which is imminent and which any one of a dozen unforeseen causes may precipitate."

About that same time, Agent Palmer at Cheyenne River reported to Washington that "there is no doubt now that the Hostile Indians at all the dancing camps are preparing to defy the authority of the Department."

On Standing Rock, Agent McLaughlin wanted no help from the army. Apparently immune to the spoils system, McLaughlin was proud of the job he had done over the years and of his record, which had won the praise of army officers as well as critics of the government's Indian policy. Past experience at his post convinced McLaughlin that he could handle any crisis without calling in outside help.

On November 16 McLaughlin, with his interpreter Louis

Primeau, visited Sitting Bull's camp on the Grand River. A Ghost Dance was in full swing. Nearly one hundred men, women, and children, intoxicated with emotion, danced around the prayer tree, while twice the number of dancers watched the ceremony from nearby. From the big tent Sitting Bull had set up, the chief directed the proceedings with the help of his assistant, Bull Ghost.

While McLaughlin and Primeau watched, a young girl dancer fell to the ground in a trance. Sitting Bull had her carried to his big tent and laid on a pile of robes. As she lay there babbling, he said she had "died," and he interpreted the conversation she was holding with dead relatives in the Spirit Land.

McLaughlin did not interfere. He spent the night in the nearby cabin of Lieutenant Bull Head. The next morning, however, McLaughlin confronted Sitting Bull as the chief emerged from a sweat bath and tried to persuade him to stop the dance.

A curious crowd gathered. It was well known among the Indians that for seven years these two men had fought a battle for power. McLaughlin was determined to win the Hunkpapas on Standing Rock over to the white man's way of life. Sitting Bull, on his part, was just as determined that the Indians should follow the old paths.

McLaughlin was insistent. The Ghost Dance must be stopped, he declared. After listening to McLaughlin for a while, Sitting Bull made a suggestion. He would travel with the agent from tribe to tribe, tracking down rumors of the prophet, journeying as far as the Rocky Mountains if necessary. If at last it was evident that there was no truth to the stories, that the prophet either did not exist or was a fake, then Sitting Bull would return to the reservation and tell his people the truth. If, on the other hand, their search revealed that the prophet did exist and that the doctrine he preached was true, then McLaughlin must stop interfering with the dance.

McLaughlin replied that such a journey would be like chasing last year's wind. He made a simple counterproposal. Sitting Bull should visit McLaughlin at the agency, and there, in one evening, McLaughlin would convince him of the foolishness of this new religion.

Sitting Bull declared solemnly that he would give McLaughlin's proposal some thought. McLaughlin withdrew and returned to the agency.

When Sitting Bull did not appear at the agency, McLaughlin counted on help from the bitter Dakota winter to put a stop to the dances. But Sitting Bull, who could read the signs of nature as well as a white man could read the Bible, saw that weather would not interfere with the dance. "Yes, my people," he told them, "you can dance all winter this year; the sun will shine warmly, and the weather will be fair." Sitting Bull had read the signs well. The winter of 1890–91 was one of the mildest on record.

McLaughlin made another suggestion to Washington. If the government did not want to arrest Sitting Bull, would the Indian Bureau give the agent permission to tell Sitting Bull's people that those who would stop dancing or would declare their opposition to the new religion could collect their rations, but those who insisted on staying with Sitting Bull would get none? McLaughlin was certain, from past experience, that most of the people would desert their chief when they grew hungry enough. By the time McLaughlin's letter reached Washington, however, the situation on the other agencies had become explosive, and the officials were considering stronger measures.

A week before McLaughlin wrote his letter to Washington, Royer lost complete control of his Pine Ridge Sioux. The incident occurred on ration day. Oglalas came in from all points of the reservation, dressed for what was for them a holiday. At noon they gathered at the corral. Royer, perhaps hoping to demonstrate his friendship to the Indians, permitted the steers to be turned loose one at a time so that the Indians could chase and shoot them as they had once hunted the buffalo. When the cattle had all been killed, the meat was dressed and divided among the people. As a result of the latest cut in rations, the meat did not go far. At the commissary, the women lined up for their meager allotments of

bacon, flour, coffee, and sugar. From there they went to the
three trading posts located on the agency and traded what
they could for more supplies. Outside the cluster of agency
buildings, dances and horse races were begun.

An Indian named Little, wanted by the police for slaugh-
tering breeding stock, strutted around the agency boasting
that the police hadn't been able to catch him. Royer sent
Lieutenant Thunder Bear and a squad of policemen to arrest
Little. They caught up with him outside a building that
housed the post dispensary and the police assembly room. In
the dispensary, Dr. Charles A. Eastman, a full-blooded Sioux,
was examining patients. Next door in the assembly room, the
Oglala headmen were holding a council.

Thunder Bear went up to Little and told him he was under
arrest. Little drew a butcher knife and dared the police to try
to take him. Ghost Dancers came flying from all directions,
brandishing guns, tomahawks, and knives and surrounding
the police. Inside the assembly room, the headmen heard the
disturbance and rushed outside. The police were seized by
the dancers, and there were angry shouts that the police
should be killed and the agency burned.

From where he stood among the group of headmen, American Horse made himself heard above the din:

> Stop! Think! What are you going to do? Kill these men of
> our own race? Then what? Kill all these helpless white men,
> women, and children? And what then? What will these brave
> words and brave deeds lead to in the end? How long can you
> hold out? Your country is surrounded with a network of rail-
> roads; thousands of white soldiers will be here within three
> days. What ammunition have you? What provisions? What
> will become of your families? Think, think, my brothers! This
> is a child's madness.

Dr. Eastman, who had come to the door of the dispensary to watch, later stated that "this man's voice had almost
magic power," and dead silence fell upon the mob.

Then Jack Red Cloud, the old chief's son, broke away from

the crowd and rushed up to American Horse brandishing a cocked pistol. "It is you and your kind who have brought us to this pass!" he yelled. American Horse turned his back on the young Indian and, with great dignity, mounted the steps to the council room and closed the door behind him.

The crowd began to move off, taking Little with them. There was nothing the police could do.

This was not the end of the Oglalas' defiance. The next day Little sent a message to Royer demanding the dismissal of all the policemen who had tried to arrest him. If this was not done, Little threatened, the agent could look for even worse trouble on the next ration day. Threats were also made against American Horse, and the chief, with his wife, moved in for a time with Dr. Eastman.

What little control Royer had exercised over the Oglalas at Pine Ridge had been destroyed. He began sending frantic telegrams to the Indian Bureau in Washington, begging permission to come to Washington, hoping that in person he could convince officials that it was imperative that troops be sent to control the Indians. "The police force are overpowered and disheartened," he complained the day after the Little affair. "We have no protection, are at the mercy of these crazy dancers."

Belt's reply was that if conditions were as bad as Royer declared them to be, it seemed hardly the time for him to leave his post and come to Washington. Still, Belt could no longer risk withholding troops from Pine Ridge. He recommended to Secretary of Interior Noble that the War Department be advised of the emergency at Pine Ridge and asked to send troops. Noble went directly to the president with the matter, and that same day the president directed the secretary of war to "assume responsibility for the suppression of any threatened outbreak, and to take such steps as may be necessary to that end." A message was sent to General Miles in Chicago, who, in turn, alerted his sub-headquarters at Omaha and St. Paul to have units ready to send to the Sioux reservations.

On November 15, before the troops could be sent, Royer,

who was unaware that his last wire had brought the results
he had hoped for, sent another telegram to Washington.
Thoroughly frightened and beside himself with frustration,
he abandoned the tone of deference that he customarily assumed in communications to his superiors. Royer's message
contained a rebuke to Washington for ignoring his past pleas
and allowing the situation to deteriorate so far. He issued a
curt prescription of what should be done.

> Indians are dancing in the snow and are wild and crazy. I
> have fully informed you that the employees and government
> property at this agency have no protection and are at the mercy
> of the Ghost Dancers. Why delay by further investigation? *We
> need protection and we need it now.* I have submitted to you
> the results of six weeks calm conservative investigation and
> nothing short of one thousand soldiers will settle this dancing.
> The leaders should be arrested and confined in some military
> post until the matter is quieted and this should be done at once.
> Royer, Agt.

Two days later General Miles instructed Brigadier General
John R. Brooke to accompany troops to Pine Ridge and Rosebud.

5

The Bluecoats Arrive

THE INDIANS' grapevine was a marvelous means of communication. No white man ever succeeded completely in figuring out how it worked. The rumor that troops were being sent to their agencies reached the Oglalas and Brules on November 19. The following morning, they awakened at dawn to find a frightening number of troops arriving. These included the Ninth Cavalry, which was made up entirely of Negro troops, whom the Indians immediately nicknamed the "buffalo soldiers" because of the buffalo-robe overcoats they wore. The Sioux had taken so much punishment from the army before they had finally surrendered and consented to live on reservations that the sight of "bluecoats" filled them with dread. Whatever defiance the Sioux had exhibited toward their agents in the decade since their surrender, they had always stopped short of provoking a crisis serious enough to require that the government send in troops. The Indians wanted no more to do with the soldiers.

Now the troops were arriving and large numbers of the Oglalas at Pine Ridge, shocked at the disaster that their activities had provoked, abandoned their homes and the dance camps and flocked into the agency to declare themselves "friendlies." Whites, too—missionaries, schoolteachers, farmers, and others who worked in the outlying reservation districts—streamed in to enjoy the security provided by the army's presence.

The Pine Ridge Agency was a village divided into two sections by a road that ran south to Rushville, Nebraska, about twenty-five miles away. On the east side of the road stood the "civilian," or public, section. In this part of the village were two churches with their parsonages—Episcopal and Presbyterian—three trading posts, and a crude hotel made from logs. The "official" portion of the agency lay on the west side of the Rushville Road. In this part were the shops, warehouses, employees' apartments, and the long building that housed the council room and offices of the agent, chief clerk, and Indian police. There were a house for the agent and his family and two schools—one a day school, the other a 180-pupil boarding school. Scattered around the outskirts of the village were the cabins of some half-breeds. Along both sides of White Clay Creek, which ran just to the east of the hamlet, Red Cloud's band had built their cabins around the imposing, two-storied frame house the government had built for Red Cloud, but in which the old chief refused to live.

Agent Royer's house was turned over to General Brooke for use as his headquarters. A tent city was quickly set up by the soldiers between the agency and the bottomlands, which were now crowded with tepees belonging to the friendlies.

Sentries were assigned to patrol the agency streets, and guards were placed at all the key buildings. General Brooke issued orders that the Oglala boarding school was to be locked up and that none of the children inside were to be allowed to leave. The teacher, Elaine Goodale, suspected the general was using the children as hostages to guarantee the good behavior of their parents.

Dr. V. T. McGillycuddy, who had been removed as agent on Pine Ridge in 1886 and replaced by a Democrat, arrived on the reservation in the winter of 1890 as a representative of the governor of Dakota. He and Red Cloud had battled often in the old days, but now Red Cloud greeted him as an old friend and admitted that if the Oglalas had listened to McGillycuddy earlier, they would not be in such grave trouble now.

"Little Beard, we have not behaved half as badly as we did in your day," the old chief told him sorrowfully,

> but you never sent for troops. Why have these soldiers been brought here, coming in the night with their big guns? It looks as if they have come to fight, and if it is so, we must fight. But we are tired of war, and we think of our women and children, and our property, our homes, our little farms, and the cattle we are raising. Can you not send these soldiers away, and if you will, we give you twenty-five of our young men you can take as hostages, and everything will be settled in one sleep.

McGillycuddy told the chief regretfully that he had no power anymore on Pine Ridge and could do nothing more than carry Red Cloud's words to the soldier chief at the agency.

General Brooke, however, was unreceptive, both to Red Cloud's message and to McGillycuddy's opinion that the trouble would end if the troops were moved over the line into Nebraska.

The next night, Young-Man-Afraid-of-His-Horses came to McGillycuddy's cabin, also asking that the former agent use his influence to have the soldiers removed. "Father, fourteen winters have passed since the Custer Massacre," the chief said.

> The children of those days are our warriors now. They do not know the power of the white man, as we older people do, and they think that they can hold their own. The troops came here, and Sitting Bull in the North at once sent his runners through

us to stir our young men up . . . unless the soldiers are taken
away, we will not be able to hold our young men.

But McGillycuddy again had to answer that his old
power had been taken from him; there was little he could
do except talk, and neither General Brooke nor Agent Royer
would listen to him.

It was McGillycuddy's opinion that the Indians should
be permitted to dance themselves out; for when spring
arrived and brought no Messiah, McGillycuddy was certain
the dance would die out. "Besides," he asked General Brooke,

> what right have we to dictate to them on a religious belief
> founded on the teaching of the religion of the white man? If the
> Seventh Day Adventists get up on the roofs of their houses, ar-
> rayed in their ascension robes, to meet the "second coming," the
> army is not rushed into their field.

While the arrival of the troops instantly dampened the
mood of revolt among hundreds of the Oglalas, it only in-
flamed the more fanatical of the Ghost Dancers. Under
Little Wound, the dancers on Medicine Root, Wounded
Knee, and White Clay creeks became more frenzied. On
Little Wound's orders, warriors—painted and dressed for
war—rode about the countryside on the nights of November 20 and 21, spreading word among the Sioux that all
the faithful who wished to continue the Ghost Dance
should assemble on White River at the mouth of White
Clay Creek.

On November 22 Census Agent A. T. Lea came into the
agency and reported that dancers were already gathering
at the place of rendezvous. The Indians declared that they
had no intention of attacking the agency but vowed that
they would defend themselves if the army attacked them.
The rebels announced that after dancing all winter, they
would go on a "big hunt" as soon as spring arrived. Lea
suspected that instead of a big hunt, they planned to go
on the warpath.

Lea reported that the Indians meant to ignore the agent and the troops. "Nor will they pay any attention to the regulations of the Department," Lea stated. "What little they get from it they can well do without." The Indians felt only contempt for the scanty rations issued them by a government that was determined to force them to farm—even if it had to starve them to do it.

In fact, the small corps of Ghost Dancers was in a good position to declare its independence of any need for rations. The herds of domestic cattle and horses had grown during the last decade to sufficient numbers to enable the rebels to feed themselves for a long time. The dancers were well armed, too. During the years of peace, they had bought or traded goods for Winchester repeating rifles from the traders and merchants of Valentine and Rushville, Nebraska, just over the reservation line.

At Rosebud the Brules were as shocked as the Oglalas had been to find troops on their reservation. Angry and feeling threatened, they fled from what they considered their prison. Eleven hundred of them headed west. Some of them, under Two Strike, went on the warpath and headed directly for the agency at Pine Ridge. Two Strike was determined to stab General Brooke as the first act of war. But he stopped at Wounded Knee Creek, only fifteen miles east of the Pine Ridge Agency.

The remainder of the fleeing Brules, led by Eagle Pipe, Turning Bear, High Hawk, Lance, No Flesh, Pine Bird, Crow Dog, and White Horse, assembled in the northwest corner of their own reservation and from there moved a little more than ten miles into the Pine Ridge Reservation and joined Short Bull's camp on Pass Creek.

During the following week, General Brooke called up heavy reinforcements. In addition to the extra regular army troops he enlisted two troops of Indian scouts, consisting of forty Oglalas and forty Cheyennes.

To the suddenly swollen population at Pine Ridge was now added a number of newspapermen whose editors had sent them to cover this new "Indian war." It was a great disappointment to most of them to discover that there was no war. Jammed into James A. Finley's tiny hotel, which was already overflowing with whites who had taken refuge in the agency, they set out to satisfy their editors, who were clamoring for thrilling war news. The newspapermen's source of stories was their own imaginations, exercised at the bar in James Asay's trading post. They filed stories about burning arrows' being fired into agency buildings, about atrocities that were being committed by the Indians, and battles that never took place, delighting their editors and the readers back home.

General Brooke was incensed to discover that the reporters were giving their readers the impression that a fierce Indian war was being waged. He banished one reporter from the agency and refused to grant any more interviews. The reporters retaliated by criticizing Brooke sharply in their columns and accusing him of appeasing the Indians. They wanted a war, and he was not providing one.

General Brooke's instructions had been to avoid a war at all costs. He had been helped in this respect by the Indians themselves. With the arrival of the troops, the Indians had instantly divided into two groups—friendlies and hostiles. Thus far, the hostiles had done nothing that would warrant sending troops against them. They were belligerent and defiant, but they had not fired a single shot nor staged a single raid. The best solution seemed to Brooke to be to try to coax the hostiles into the agency, where the whole matter could be ironed out.

Brooke's plan was partially successful. Two chiefs, Little Wound and Big Road, brought their bands into the agency. But Short Bull and Kicking Bear, the two passionate apostles of the Ghost Dance, refused to come in. On November 25 Short Bull had broken up his dance camp on Pass Creek and moved it to the mouth of White Clay Creek, where he joined forces with Kicking Bear and his followers. Two Strike, who had vowed to kill General Brooke, was still hesitating on Wounded Knee Creek. The composition of these two groups was largely Brule. Most Oglalas had left their dance camps and gone into the agency.

On November 30 the groups headed by Short Bull, Two Strike, and Kicking Bear headed for a rendezvous at the mouth of Grass Creek. Along the way, each group looted the cabins and rounded up the beef cattle of their brothers who had gone into the agency. In addition, Short Bull's band raided the agency herd camp across from the mouth of Willow Creek. The chief herder estimated the number of raiders at one thousand men.

These combined forces continued a short distance down the White River and then turned northward. Their destination was a level, elevated plateau that thrust up between the White and Cheyenne rivers. The Indians were thoroughly familiar with the plateau. Now called the Cuny Table, it offered an unassailable place of refuge. It rose several hundred feet above the prairie, and there were few approaches to its steep sides. From its northeast edge, a strip of land jutted out, ending in a small, flat triangle of land about three miles long at the sides and two miles wide at the base. The Indians called this smaller table of land the Stronghold. Two springs provided it with water, and there was sufficient grass upon it for their stock. The strip of land that connected these two plateaus was scarcely wider than a wagon. Given these features, the Stronghold was a natural fortress. Even an army the size of the one Brooke had gathered would have a difficult time waging a successful assault against it.

Sending out scouts to provide ample warning in case of attack, the rebels resumed their dancing with renewed frenzy. The dancers thought it more urgent than ever before to usher in the new world.

Meanwhile, in Chicago and Washington, a new move to bring the situation under control was being considered. Commissioner Belt was advocating the arrest of the dance leaders, a suggestion he had rejected earlier when it had been made by Agents McLaughlin and Royer. But now that the army was present on the reservations and could make the arrests, Belt pushed the proposal. Furthermore, any protests from critics of the government's inhumane policy toward the Indians would be directed, not at the Indian Bureau, but at the army.

In his headquarters at Chicago, General Miles also thought the arrest of the dance leaders was a good idea. However, the situation on both Pine Ridge and Rosebud was at the moment too explosive to make such a move. At Standing Rock conditions were better. McLaughlin still had his Indians under control. Miles believed it would be possible to arrest Sitting Bull and remove him from the reservation. To Miles, as to most of the American public, no other chief so fully personified the spirit of Indian resistance. The general was convinced that the Hunkpapa chief was at the bottom of the whole Ghost Dance rebellion.

McLaughlin advised against an immediate arrest. He urged that such a move be put off until winter. With the arrival of the snows and the bitter cold, the Indians customarily became languid and inactive. It would be easier then to make the arrest with a minimum of resistance. McLaughlin also advised that, since the appearance of white soldiers would be bound to excite the Indians, the arrest be made by Indian policemen. His suggestions were supported by General Ruger and Colonel Drum.

General Miles had only contempt for Indian agents— an opinion with a firm basis in some instances, but not in the case of McLaughlin. Miles paid no attention to McLaughlin's advice, and when he encountered William F. Cody, an old friend, at a banquet on November 24, an idea struck him. Buffalo Bill Cody had served as scout for Miles during the general's campaign against Sitting Bull in 1876. Later, Sitting Bull had been a featured attraction of Cody's famous Wild West Show for a season. Cody was just the man, Miles decided, to send out after Sitting Bull.

Always the showman, Buffalo Bill couldn't resist the

chance to add the arrest of Sitting Bull to his list of achievements. Besides, the Ghost Dance and the troubled Sioux were front-page news. If Buffalo Bill succeeded in arresting the chief, it would mean enormous publicity for his Wild West Show.

Miles provided Cody with a written order for the arrest of the Hunkpapa chief and instructions for military commanders along the way to provide whatever transportation Cody might need. The old scout started on his mission at once, without taking time to change clothes or to pack a bag.

Cody arrived at Standing Rock on the evening of November 27 with an entourage of eight men. Five of the eight were reporters. The other three—Frank Powell (White Beaver), Robert Haslam (Pony Bob), and G. W. Cadwick—were friends Cody had stopped to pick up in Wisconsin. Cody appeared before McLaughlin and presented his credentials, still wearing the dress suit and patent leather slippers he had worn to the banquet in Chicago.

Although he said nothing, McLaughlin disapproved of the plan. Both he and Colonel Drum were convinced that if Cody tried to carry out his mission he might get himself killed and trigger an outbreak as well. To gain time the two men invited the famous scout to enjoy himself at the officers' club at Fort Yates for the rest of the evening. They hoped to get him drunk and delay him long enough to get the order canceled. As soon as Cody had left for the officers' club, McLaughlin fired off a telegram to Washington.

Late the next morning, Cody walked out of the club— little the worse for wear—and set off with his entourage and a wagonload of presents, largely candy and sweets, for Sitting Bull's camp. Just before leaving, Cody gave the eager reporters at the agency a news story about the intended plan, calling it "the most dangerous undertaking of my career." The statement was pure showmanship, however, for he expected no trouble from his old friend.

No reply to McLaughlin's wire to Washington had been

received, but the agent and Colonel Drum had taken other steps. Mysterious messages had been sent out by fast-riding couriers to several points on the reservation during the night.

Cody and his friends rode twenty miles the first day and camped for the night at the place where Sitting Bull Road crossed Oak Creek. Louis Primeau, the interpreter, rode into camp the next morning and asked where Cody was headed. After Cody replied, Primeau informed him that he was too late. "Sitting Bull has gone into the agency with Jack Carignan. They went over the other trail," said Primeau.

Carignan taught in a school three miles from Sitting Bull's camp and served as a spy for McLaughlin. To an inquiry from McLaughlin, Carignan had replied during the night that the Sioux were quieter. Carignan reported that the Indians were "dancing still at Sitting Bull's, but not in such numbers, owing to the fact that Male Bear has started a dance on Little Oak Creek. . . . The Indians seem to be very peaceably inclined, and I do not apprehend any trouble."

McLaughlin had heard a rumor that Indians from Standing Rock were en route to Pine Ridge and asked Carignan if it was true. Carignan replied in the same letter that he knew of no Indian movement from Grand River.

> The Indians have been told that the Soldiers are coming down here, and are badly frightened. If they were assured different there would be no danger of any of them leaving. I have done all I could in telling them that the reports they have heard are all lies, and that no one would try to prevent them from dancing. I am positive that no trouble need be apprehended from Sitting Bull and his followers, unless they are forced to defend themselves and think it would be advisable to keep all strangers, other than employees, who have business amongst the Indians away from here.

William Cody was hardly a stranger to Sitting Bull, but, on the other hand, his mission was not a friendly one. It seemed advisable to prevent Cody from trying to see Sitting Bull.

When Cody expressed doubts about the validity of Primeau's story, the interpreter suggested they ride over to the other trail and search for signs. There they found tracks indicating that two ponies, one shod and one unshod, had recently pulled a buggy over the trail.

Disappointed that he would not be the one to arrest the famous chief, Cody returned to the agency, only to discover that the trail had been faked and that he had been deceived. Whatever fury Cody might have felt was dampened by a telegram McLaughlin showed him. It had been received by Colonel Drum from department headquarters only four hours after Cody and his party had started for Grand River. As a result of McLaughlin's hurried wire to Washington, the president himself had suspended Cody's orders. There was nothing for Cody to do but return to Chicago.

General Miles was furious over the episode, and it reinforced his opinion that the agents were not qualified to run the agencies. Miles pressed for army control of the reservations and for restoration of the full rations guaranteed the Indians by treaty. The Sioux were starving, he said, and filling their stomachs would ease much of the tension that now existed on the reservations. On November 28 Miles started for Washington to use personal persuasion to win acceptance of his proposals.

Miles's suggestions provoked much argument in Washington. Officials of the Indian Bureau had so far ignored most of the evidence that the Indians were starving because of the ration cuts made by the House of Representatives. Acting Commissioner Belt called Miles's statements "exaggerated and unfounded." If the Sioux were hungry, Belt insisted, it was because of their own laziness and stubborn refusal to farm.

But another voice spoke out for the Indians. Congress had just convened when Miles reached Washington, and a bill was introduced to provide federal arms and ammunition for the terrified settlers near the Sioux reservations. During the debate over this bill, Senator Daniel Voorhees arose and denounced the bill and the muddleheaded thinking that had given rise to it.

> I look upon the policy which has been pursued by the administration of Indian affairs as a crime revolting to man and God. I look upon the present outbreak or threatened outbreak—which will bring not merely the destruction of the Indians, but will bathe the snows of the Northwest crimson with the blood of our own brave soldiers and officers—as something revolting in the extreme, and that instead of sitting here debating Election bills and Force bills, and providing for the issuance of arms to the States in the Northwest, we should be hurrying, anxiously and eagerly, to provide for the feeding of these starving people.

But Voorhees's words had no effect upon a Congress that had consistently refused to see the Indian as a human being. Arms were given the settlers, while no action was taken in the House on a bill that would have appropriated money to supply the Indians with more food.

The secretary of the interior, however, followed General Miles's advice and ordered the Sioux agents to buy all the food for the Indians that they had been promised by treaty, even though it meant spending money that was supposed to last for the next six months.

On his other proposal—that the reservations be taken away from the Department of the Interior and be placed under the jurisdiction of the army—Miles won a partial victory. The secretary ordered the commissioner of Indian affairs to wire the Sioux agents that they were to "cooperate with and obey the orders of the military officer commanding on the reservation in your charge."

The order came too late to stop Agent A. P. Dixon from acting on his own to put a quick damper on the Ghost Dance craze that threatened to take hold of the Crow Creek and Lower Brule reservations. The smallest of the Sioux reservations, the Crow Creek and Lower Brule were separated by the Missouri River but administered by the same agent. Until late November, there was no sign that the Indians living there were going to join with their brothers on the other reservations in dancing a new world into being. The Lower Yanktonais at Crow Creek—east of the river—had accepted the inevitable and become the Christianized tillers of the soil the American government stubbornly insisted they become. The Lower Yanktonais scorned the new religion their brothers were embracing so fervently. The Lower Brules, although no longer as militant as their kinsmen to the south on the Rosebud, had never been satisfied with the boundaries drawn for them under the land agreement. They had been pressing for permission to move down to the Rosebud and live with the Upper Brules and were seething with anger because Commissioner Belt refused to allow it. When some of the Ghost Dance apostles appeared at the Lower Brule camps in late November, they quickly made some converts to the new religion.

On November 27, the same day Buffalo Bill Cody arrived at Standing Rock to attempt an arrest of Sitting Bull, Agent Dixon learned that a dance was to be held on his reservation. He moved swiftly, and by the next evening he had nine dance leaders in his tiny jail and had sent a wire to Washington requesting help in finding a place to hold the rest of the dancers that he planned to take into custody. Twenty-two arrests were made in the next several days. Soldiers arrived to take seventeen of the prisoners to Fort Snelling, Minnesota.

When word of Agent Dixon's actions reached Belt in Washington, the acting commissioner was dismayed. He wanted to keep his and the department's hands clean of the whole affair and to let any blame or criticism fall on the army. On December 6 Belt telegraphed: "Secretary directs that you make no more arrests whatever except under orders of the military or upon an order of the Secretary of the Interior."

But there was no need for any more arrests or any further action. As a result of Agent Dixon's prompt exercise of his authority, the Ghost Dance movement on the Lower Brule Reservation died a quick death. It never came to life again.

Having been given the power to handle the rebellion in his own way, General Miles set out to dissipate the strength of the dancers on the Cheyenne River Reservation. He thought he knew how it could be done. In the absence of Kicking Bear, who had fled to the Stronghold, the Miniconjou dancers looked to Hump and Big Foot for leadership. They had gathered together in one huge camp on the Cheyenne River near the mouth of Cherry Creek. As many as six hundred people kept a dance going almost continuously. Across the river, just outside the reservation, the new settlement of Cheyenne City felt threatened. Its less than twenty settlers feared being attacked at any moment.

Inside the reservation, Narcisse Narcelle, a mixed-blood whose ranch was only a few miles from the dance camp, was trying to persuade the two chiefs that this new religion was nonsense. He found a receptive listener in Hump, who had thrown off his police uniform in September to lead a group of dancers, but whose faith in the new religion had begun to weaken. Persuading Big Foot to give up the Ghost Dance was another matter. Not only did he continue to encourage his people to dance, he urged them to get hold of all the guns and ammunition they could find. When Agent Palmer visited the camp on November 27, friendly Indians warned him that the dancers planned to go on the warpath soon.

General Miles knew Hump well. The chief had surrendered to the general in 1877 and had afterward served him faithfully as a scout during the Nez Percé war of 1877. Miles thought that there was a good chance that Hump could be persuaded to quit the Cherry Creek camp and bring his people back into the agency. Miles hoped to accomplish Hump's "conversion" through an officer named Ezra P.

Ewers, a captain with the Fifth Infantry who had had charge of Hump and his band for seven years and had gained their full confidence and respect. Ewers was at the time on duty in Texas, but upon receiving orders from Miles, he started for Sioux country. Upon his arrival there, he reported to Fort Bennett on the west side of the Missouri River just below the Cheyenne River Agency. Although Ewers was warned that Hump and his dancers were considered extremely dangerous, he left the fort at once, taking with him only Lieutenant Harry C. Hale. After a ride of sixty miles, they reached the dance camp. Hump was not there. He was twenty miles away, but a runner was sent for him. When the chief learned that his friend Captain Ewers had come to visit him, he returned immediately to his camp.

Persuading the chief to turn from the new religion was easier than Captain Ewers or even Miles had expected it to be. Hump, when informed that General Miles wanted him to give up the dance and bring his people to the agency, replied that he would do as the general wished. Not all of his people followed him, but on December 9 Hump arrived at the Cheyenne River Agency with most of his band. Once more he put on his police uniform and began trying to persuade the other dance leaders to do as he had done.

Much of Big Foot's enthusiasm for the dance cooled when he saw his friend reject it and return to the agency. Big Foot led his people home to their cabins at the mouth of Deep Creek.

Since spring an army "camp of observation" had been located a few miles west of Big Foot's camp. On December 7, Colonel H. C. Merriam and the Seventh Infantry had reached Fort Sully on the east bank of the Missouri just below the Cheyenne River Agency. Merriam and his men made preparations to cross the Missouri and proceed up the Cheyenne toward Big Foot's camp. A week later the "camp of observation" was reinforced by another company of infantry and a detachment of Indian scouts. When the

commander of the camp, Lieutenant Colonel Edwin V.
Sumner, visited Big Foot after the chief's arrival home,
Big Foot declared that he did not intend to make any
trouble. All indications are that the chief was telling the
truth.

The situation on the Cheyenne River Reservation appeared to have been brought under control. Rosebud, too, was
quiet. The hostiles had fled to the Stronghold, leaving only
friendlies at the agency. Agent Wright had returned to
Rosebud on December 1, cleared of the charges brought
against him in September in the matter of the Indian rations.
Special Agent Reynolds, who had been filling in for Wright,
stayed on to help. Upon Wright's return to the agency, a
delegation of friendlies called upon him to assure him they
wanted only peace. They voiced sharp disapproval of their
brothers who had fortified themselves on the Stronghold,
but they begged Wright not to let the dreaded soldiers
harm them. Wright quieted the Indians' fears as best he
could, but he was no longer in full charge of his agency.
He was under orders to obey the military commander on
his reservation in regard to any action taken against the
hostiles.

A crisis still existed at Pine Ridge. The village had become
a city. Only a few of the Oglalas had accompanied Short
Bull and Kicking Bear to the Stronghold. The rest had come
into the agency. It was estimated that there were now more
than four thousand frightened, restless, and suspicious Indians crowding about the agency. Many of the dancers who
had been forced to return were still believers in the strange
religion, but they had come to the agency because they were
afraid of what the soldiers might do if they didn't cooperate.
To isolate the believers from the nonbelievers and so keep
a better eye on potential troublemakers, Brooke had the Indians separated into different camps.

Yet it was the Brules and the Oglalas on the Stronghold
who caused General Brooke the gravest concern. When the

huge dance camp on White Clay Creek had broken up and
had begun to move under the leadership of Short Bull and
Kicking Bear, Brooke had become alarmed. He feared the
Indians were heading for Canada, thus endangering the
Black Hills settlements. It came as something of a relief to
Brooke, therefore, when the Indians stopped at the Stronghold. Word was sent to the agency that they meant to stay
where they were and dance all winter. In the meantime,
they would decide what they wanted to do when spring
arrived. They warned the general to leave them alone and
declared that they would fight to the last man if the army
tried to force them from the Stronghold. Brooke took them
at their word.

Rejecting the possibility of dislodging the hostiles by direct military assault, the general opted for diplomacy. He
sent several large parties of friendlies to the Stronghold to
try to persuade their brothers to come into the agency. Each
time the friendlies approached the plateau, they were fired
upon by pickets stationed around the Stronghold and turned
back. Then Brooke remembered Father John Jutz, the sev-
enty-year-old Catholic missionary whom the Indians loved.
He had come to Pine Ridge in 1888 to establish the Holy
Rosary Mission and School, four miles north of the agency.
With Franciscan Sisters from Buffalo, New York, as teachers,
the mission had attracted many converts, and Father Jutz
had won the love and respect of the Brules. They had once
promised him that if war should come, neither he nor any
who sought refuge in his mission would be harmed. When
Brooke suggested to the missionary that he might be able
to enter the Stronghold, Father Jutz agreed.

At noon on December 3, the priest set out for the dance
camp. He was accompanied by Jack Red Cloud, who until
quite recently had been one of the Ghost Dance leaders. The
next day, ten miles from the Stronghold, they encountered
the picket line that curved around the tiny plateau. One of
the pickets rode back into camp to confer with Short Bull.

Not long afterward, he returned with word that Father Jutz
was to be admitted.

At eleven o'clock that night, Father Jutz and Jack Red
Cloud arrived at Short Bull's headquarters. Waiting with
Short Bull were Kicking Bear, Two Strike, Turning Bear, High
Hawk, Crow Dog, Eagle Pipe, and several others. The chiefs
listened politely to Father Jutz's plea that they give up the
dance and return to the agency. Then they began enumerat-
ing their grievances. They were irate over the latest census
report, which claimed that there were two thousand fewer
Indians at Rosebud than there formerly were. This was not
true, they declared bitterly, and they therefore were not
being given enough food. The Indians at the agency were
hungry; some of them were actually starving. The hostiles
were also angry about a change that had been made in the
boundary between Rosebud and Pine Ridge.

When the Indians got around to replying to Father Jutz's
plea to surrender, they declared they could see no good reason to do so. Because they had driven their breeding stock
to the Stronghold and were butchering the cattle, they were
no longer hungry. In addition, they were certain that they
would be arrested if they returned to the agency. They said
they would rather die fighting than be locked up in the white
man's prisons.

The council went on all night. By daybreak, Father Jutz
had persuaded several of the leaders to at least come in to
talk with General Brooke. The delegation, consisting of Two
Strike, Turning Bear, Big Turkey, High Pine, Big-Bad-Horse,
and Bull Dog, with an escort of twenty-four armed warriors,
set off almost immediately. All of the hostiles were painted
for war. They had woven sacred eagle feathers into their
own hair and into the manes and tails of their ponies. A few
wore their Ghost Shirts. Even Father Jutz had not been able
to convince them that there would be no trouble, and they
were prepared for it. They were so nervous that, several
times during the journey, the column broke into milling confusion over harmless and trivial incidents.

It took the party two days to reach Father Jutz's mission. There they camped for the night, and upon either Father Jutz's advice or their own judgment, they proceeded the next morning to the agency, washed clean of war paint and minus eagle feathers. Bearing a white flag, they moved, still apprehensive, toward the agency. Behind the mounted warriors, Two Strike rode in a buggy with Father Jutz. Four times the procession hesitated, suspicious and fearful of what awaited them. It was only Father Jutz's guarantee that the Indians could kill him if the soldiers tried to arrest them that finally moved the procession forward.

Somewhat reassured, the Indians marched into the agency, dismounted with military precision before Brooke's headquarters, and followed Father Jutz inside with the extraordinary dignity Indians can exhibit on certain occasions.

Word had been sent by Father Jutz that the chiefs were coming to the agency, and in the small headquarters building, preparations had been made. The chiefs were seated with proper ceremony in a semicircle of chairs. General Brooke then took a seat facing them. With him were Colonel Frank Wheaton and Colonel James Forsyth.

The general urged the chiefs to surrender and make peace. The chiefs replied with a long list of grievances their people had suffered under the white man's domination. They asked for assurance that these injustices would be corrected before they once again asked their people to give up their freedom. Brooke replied that the Indians must surrender first, and then their complaints would be dealt with. There was one action, however, that Brooke could take immediately. He could provide all the food they and their people needed. They would no longer have to butcher their breeding stock to feed themselves. In addition, he would give some of their young men jobs as scouts.

Turning Bear rose to speak for the Indians. As there was no enemy, he said, he could see no reason why the soldier chief needed scouts. Still, the young men would be glad to earn some money. But coming to the agency would require much thought. There were already so many Indians camped around the agency that there was neither grass nor water enough for the ponies and cattle the Stronghold Indians would bring in. And transporting the older people would be a problem. They had no ponies to ride, and there were not enough ponies to pull the wagons.

When he had finished recounting the problems that would have to be solved before he and the others could bring their people in, Turning Bear said he hoped that he and his party would be given something to eat before they began the long journey back to the Stronghold.

Brooke replied that a feast had already been prepared for them and escorted them to the warehouse, where they were fed and entertained with a squaw dance. The general believed that he had succeeded in persuading the hostiles to leave the Stronghold. He wired Miles that the chiefs had agreed to come in. But he was mistaken.

The chiefs started back to the Stronghold without having made a decision. They had been impressed, however, by the cordial reception they had been given at the agency. Accompanying them when they left was a half-breed scout, Louis Shangreau, and thirty-two friendlies, who hoped to pick up any information that might prove useful and perhaps also to sway some of the other hostiles. When the Indians arrived at the Stronghold, they found a Ghost Dance in progress. The dancers refused to halt the dance to grant Shangreau a council. It was not until thirty hours later that Short Bull called an intermission to listen to what Shangreau had to say.

"The agent would forgive you if you returned now and would give you more rations," the scout informed them, "but [he would] not permit you to dance."

Crow Dog and Two Strike spoke sharply against surrender. While Two Strike had been parlaying with Brooke at the agency with the other chiefs, several members of his band had visited a trading post on Cheyenne River. Several cowboys had for no reason opened fire on the Indians, killing one.

As far as Two Strike was concerned, the blandishments Brooke had offered were nullified by this wanton killing.

But it was Short Bull who replied for the entire camp.

> I have risen today to tell you something of importance. You have heard the words of the brothers from the agency camps, and if you have done as myself, you have weighed them carefully. If the Great Father would permit us to continue the dance, would give more rations, and quit taking away portions of the reservation, I would be in favor of returning. But even if you say that he will, how can we discern whether you are telling the truth? We have been lied to so many times that we will not believe any words that your agent sends us. If we return he will take away our guns and ponies, put some of us in jail for stealing cattle and plundering houses. We prefer to stay here and die, if necessary. . . . We are free now and have plenty of beef, can dance all the time in obedience to the command of Great Wakan Tanka. We tell you to return to your agent and say to him that the Lakotas in the Badlands are not going to come in.

Short Bull directed the dance to resume, and for two days more, Shangreau could not persuade the chiefs to hold another council. But he did not sit by doing nothing. He talked to the chiefs individually, and finally—at noon on the third day—another council was called. It was obvious at once that Shangreau had had some success. Two Strike rose and for some reason reversed his previous stand, announcing that he would take his people into the agency. Crow Dog announced that he would do the same.

Angered at these desertions, Short Bull leaped to his feet and shouted:

> At such a time as this we should all stick together like brothers. Do not leave; remain with us. These men from the agency are not telling the truth; they will conduct you back to the agency and place you in jail there. Louis is at the bottom of this affair. I know he is a traitor. Kill him, kill him!

Some of the apostle's warriors sprang toward the scout, holding their rifles as clubs. The friendlies leaped to shield him with their bodies, and Two Strike's men rushed to the rescue. The whole camp erupted into action. Men, mounted and on foot, dashed about wildly, yelling, firing arrows and rifles, swinging clubs. Several fell, dead or wounded.

Crow Dog, who had an instinct for drama, suddenly sat down in the midst of the melee and drew his blanket over his head. Gradually the frenzied warriors grew quiet, their eyes on this chief who had done such an unexpected thing. When he knew that he had their complete attention, Crow Dog lifted his voice and declared despairingly that he could not bear to see Sioux kill Sioux. Then, rising with studied dignity, he announced, "I am going back to Pine Ridge; you can kill me if you want to, now, and prevent my starting. The agent's words are true, and it is better to return than to stay here. I am not afraid to die."

The chief's bravery and his determined announcement had a sobering effect upon the whole camp. Those who wished to accompany Crow Dog and Two Strike were permitted to strike their lodges and set out for the agency with Shangreau and the friendlies. Over half the camp decided to leave. Before they were two miles away, the rest of the dancers, demoralized by the sudden split, struck their lodges, too, and hurried after their kinsmen. The change of heart experienced by Short Bull and Kicking Bear was short-lived, however. They had gone only a few miles when they and two hundred diehards turned back to the Stronghold.

6

The Tragedy of Sitting Bull

AT STANDING Rock, Agent McLaughlin was worried. Although General Miles had been persuaded that Sitting Bull should be arrested, McLaughlin didn't like the idea that the army would be making the arrest. He didn't believe that the general, far away in his headquarters in Chicago, could be as aware of the delicate balance of the situation on the reservation as was McLaughlin himself. McLaughlin was convinced that the safest time to attempt the arrest was after the snows had arrived. Miles believed it was imperative that Sitting Bull be put behind bars as quickly as could be arranged.

McLaughlin also feared that the general would insist that soldiers from nearby Fort Yates make the arrest. Always fearful of the bluecoats, the dancers were now in such an emotional state that the mere appearance of soldiers, regardless of their mission, would, in McLaughlin's opinion, spark an explosion of violence. Indian police, on the other hand, might be able to make the arrest without provoking a fight.

With Colonel Drum, the commander of Fort Yates, who

shared McLaughlin's belief that the agent on the scene could determine the best time to make the arrest, McLaughlin drew up a plan. The Indian police would move into Sitting Bull's settlement at dawn on one of the biweekly ration days, when most of the Indians would be at the agency. Troops from Fort Yates would have already arrived under cover of darkness to take up a position within supporting distance. The police would make the arrest, and if a fight started, the troops would come to the rescue.

While preparations were made at the fort with a great deal of attendant secrecy so that the spies for Sitting Bull would suspect nothing, McLaughlin set about increasing the size of the police force. He could do this easily without arousing suspicion because for weeks the police had been cutting and hauling logs to build a halfway shelter where the road from Standing Rock to Grand River crossed Oak Creek. McLaughlin simply announced that he needed more men to help build the shelter and hired twenty-one additional police. These he placed under Lieutenant Bull Head and Sergeant Shave Head.

While awaiting McLaughlin's orders to make the arrest, Bull Head and his men kept watch on Sitting Bull's camp and reported to John M. Carignan, who taught in the school three miles from the chief's settlement. Carignan, in turn, reported to McLaughlin.

The cold weather McLaughlin had been waiting for finally arrived, and on December 5 it began to snow. The next day was ration day, and most of the Indians would be at the agency. To McLaughlin the circumstances appeared ideal, and he decided to try once again to get permission to arrest the chief. He wired Washington: "Everything quiet at present; weather cold and snowing. Am I authorized to arrest Sitting Bull and other fomenters of mischief when I think best?"

McLaughlin received a reply that same day: "Secretary directs that you make no arrests whatever except under orders of the military or upon an order of the Secretary of the Interior."

It was not at all what McLaughlin wanted to hear.

About this time Sitting Bull received an invitation from the dancers on the Stronghold. Short Bull informed him that because the whites were interfering so much, the Messiah was coming sooner than he had at first announced. Short Bull believed that the great chief, Sitting Bull, should be on hand to greet the Messiah when the glorious moment arrived. Sitting Bull called a council and was urged by his headmen to go. He said he would ask McLaughlin for the necessary pass, without which no Indian was supposed to leave his own reservation.

Perhaps Bull Head and his spies learned of this invitation. At any rate, the next day, December 11, Running Hawk, one of the policemen, arrived in Sitting Bull's camp with a letter from McLaughlin. The message was curt. It ordered the dancers to break up the dance camp and return to their farms. Running Hawk also warned the chief and his sub-lieutenants that the authorities planned to disarm the dancers and take away their ponies.

Sitting Bull decided to ask for a pass and reply to the message in a single letter. That night, around another council fire, Sitting Bull dictated a letter to his son-in-law, Andrew Fox, who had been to the agency school and knew some English.

"I wish to write a few lines today and let you know something," the chief began.

I held a meeting with all my Indians today, and am writing to you this message. God made you—made all the white race, and also made the Red race—and gave them both might and heart to know everything in the world, but gave the whites the advantage over the Indians. But today God, our Father, is helping us Indians, so all we Indians believe.

Therefore I think this way: I wish no man to come to me in my prayers [dances] with gun or knife. Therefore all the In-

dians pray to God for life, and try to find out a good road, and
do nothing wrong in their life. This is what we want, and to pray
to God. But you did not believe us.

You should say nothing against our religion, for we said
nothing against yours. You pray to God. So do all of us Indians,
as well as the whites. We both pray to only one God, who made
us all.

Yet you, my friend, you today think I am a fool, and you gather
up some of the wise men among my people on your side, and
you let the white people back East know what you think. I
know that, but do not object; I overlook that, because I am foolish enough to pray to God.

Therefore, my friend, you don't like me. Well, my friend, I
don't like it myself when someone is foolish. You are the same.
You don't like me because you think I am a fool, and you imagine
that, if I were not here, all the Indians would become civilized,
and that, because I am here, all the Indians are fools. I know
this is what you publish in the newspapers back East. I see it
all in the paper, but I overlook that.

When you were here in my camp, you gave me good words
about my prayers, but today you take it all back again. And
there is something else I want you to know. I am obliged to go
to Pine Ridge Agency and investigate this Ghost Dance religion.
So I write to let you know that.

The policeman told me you intend to take all our ponies, and
our guns too. So I wish you would let me know about that.
Please answer soon.

signed—Sitting Bull

Bull Ghost, a member of the chief's personal bodyguard,
rode to the agency and delivered the letter into McLaughlin's
hands on the evening of the twelfth. Only a few hours earlier,
McLaughlin had received another message. Colonel Drum
had received a wire in cipher from General Ruger. The message instructed Colonel Drum to "make it your especial duty
to secure the person of Sitting Bull. Call on Indian agent to
cooperate and render such assistance as will best promote
the purpose in view." Drum went immediately to the agency
to confer with McLaughlin, and the two men decided to
carry out the plan that they had worked out earlier. They

would execute the plan on December 20, the next ration day—with Indian police, not army troops.

For a long time Bull Head and some of his hand-picked police had been urging McLaughlin to arrest Sitting Bull and some of his headmen. There was a great deal of animosity between the dancers and those Indians friendly to the agent and the government. The police claimed they could not pass through Sitting Bull's camp without being insulted by his followers. They were eager to retaliate.

Sitting Bull's letter to McLaughlin was discomfiting. While the Indians sat waiting for McLaughlin to issue the chief a pass, the agent contemplated this latest development. The last thing in the world McLaughlin wanted was for Sitting Bull to join the dancers on the Stronghold. Short Bull and Kicking Bear were simply apostles of a new religion. Since the death of Crazy Horse, Sitting Bull had taken his place as the greatest chief among the Sioux. If he succeeded in reaching the Stronghold, his presence might have an incendiary effect upon the thousands of Sioux gathered around the agency professing friendliness. The carefully controlled situation on Pine Ridge might fall apart, and General Brooke could find himself faced with a full-scale war.

Sitting Bull was not issued a pass. McLaughlin sent Bull Ghost back to his chief with an evasive answer.

Sitting Bull's letter did not say when he planned to leave for Pine Ridge, and McLaughlin sent a quick note to Lieutenant Bull Head on Grand River alerting the lieutenant that Sitting Bull might try to leave the reservation. McLaughlin emphasized that Bull Head was to keep a close watch on the chief's camp for any such move. He was to gather in all the policemen who were strung out along Grand River under pretext of beginning construction of the halfway shelter on Oak Creek. McLaughlin warned Bull Head that if Sitting Bull tried to leave, "you must stop him and if he does not listen to you, do as you see fit, use your own discretion in the matter and it will be all right."

That night McLaughlin also sent Sergeant Shave Head, who happened to be at the agency, with a verbal message to

Bull Head, informing him that orders had been issued for the arrest of Sitting Bull. But McLaughlin instructed the Indian lieutenant "not to attempt to make the arrest until further ordered *unless* it was discovered that Sitting Bull was preparing to leave the Reservation." Shave Head took a few agency policemen with him, and the next morning eight more men, under Sergeant John Eagle Man, left the agency, supposedly to help build the shelter on Oak Creek.

That same day, Saturday, December 13, Bull Head learned that Sitting Bull's headmen had decided their chief should go to Pine Ridge despite the fact he had no pass. They began making preparations to leave on Monday, December 15. As soon as Bull Head received this information, he went to John Carignan and had him write a report to McLaughlin. The message was given to Hawk Man, one of the policemen, who started off on the forty-mile ride.

The next afternoon, Colonel Drum saw Hawk Man ride into the agency on a lathered pony and went immediately to McLaughlin's office to learn what news the Indian carried. Colonel Drum and the agent read Carignan's report together. It revealed what Bull Head had learned about Sitting Bull's latest plans.

> He [Sitting Bull] has been fitting up his horses to stand a long ride and will go horseback in case he is pursued. Bull Head would like to arrest him at once before he has a chance of giving them the slip, as he thinks that if he gets the start, it will be impossible to catch him. He says to send word to him by courier immediately.

Drum and McLaughlin realized they could not, as they had planned, wait until the next ration day to arrest Sitting Bull. It must be done immediately. They sent the following instructions back to Bull Head:

> From report brought by Scout Hawk Man, I believe that the time has arrived for the arrest of Sitting Bull and it can be made

by the Indian police without much risk. I therefore desire you to make the arrest before daylight tomorrow or as soon thereafter as possible. The Cavalry will leave tonight and reach the Sitting Bull road crossing of Oak Creek by daylight tomorrow morning (Monday), where they will remain until they hear from you.

Louis Primeau will accompany the Cavalry command as guide, and I desire you to send a messenger to the Cavalry as soon as you can after making the arrest, so that the troops may know how to act in aiding you or preventing any attempt of his followers from rescuing him.

I have ordered all the police at Oak Creek to proceed to Carignan's school and await your orders. This gives you a force of 42 policemen for the arrest.

> Very respectfully,
> James McLaughlin
> U.S. Indian Agent.

P.S. You must not let him escape under any circumstances.

Two copies of this message—one in English, the other in Sioux—were entrusted to Second Sergeant Red Tomahawk. Another messenger was sent to John Carignan, informing him of the plan.

John Lone Man, one of the Indian police, received word of the impending arrest on the morning of December 14. He was busy mending his saddle at his home on Grand River, about thirty-six miles south of Standing Rock Agency, when a fellow policeman, Charles Afraid-of-Hawk, arrived with the message that all members of the entire Indian police force had been ordered to report immediately to Lieutenant Bull Head's place, thirty miles up the river west from Lone Man's cabin.

Lone Man asked his friend what was happening, and Afraid-of-Hawk voiced his suspicion that they might be ordered to arrest Sitting Bull.

Lone Man, who had tried hard to reform and live as the white men said he must, expressed his impatience. "That is just what I expected all the time—something unpleasant would be the outcome of this Messiah craze."

Lone Man invited the other policeman to dinner, and when Lone Man's wife learned that her husband was to report with all the other police to Bull Head's house, she grew nervous, suspecting that there would be serious trouble.

After dinner, Lone Man bade goodbye to his wife and children and left with Afraid-of-Hawk for Bull Head's place. They reached their destination between six and seven o'clock that evening. Bull Head, a relative of Lone Man, greeted his kinsman warmly. Other members of the police began to arrive. When Sergeant Shave Head and High Eagle were seen approaching, Bull Head went out to greet them. High Eagle and Bull Head had been close friends since boyhood.

The two men greeted each other with hands clasped and arms locked. Bull Head said, "So, brother, you are going to be with me again."

High Eagle replied, "Wherever you go—I shall always follow you, even unto death."

Bull Head said, "Good."

By one o'clock the next morning, thirty policemen and John Carignan had assembled at Bull Head's cabin, only three miles from Sitting Bull's camp. To reach Bull Head's cabin, Carignan, accompanied by two policemen, had had to pass through the chief's village. The camp was silent—the Ghost Dance had ended for the day—but the embers of the fires still glowed. Hearing the approach of Carignan's buggy, dogs began to bark. One sleepy Indian emerged from his lodge to question the travelers. He did not recognize them in the darkness and accepted their story that they were headed for the agency.

After a hot meal, Bull Head informed his fellow policemen that he had orders from McLaughlin to arrest Sitting Bull. So that everyone would understand fully what the orders were, he had Chaska, the local interpreter, read the copy of the order in the Sioux language that McLaughlin had thought to enclose.

Lone Man recalled that all of the Indians felt sad to think that their chief, with his followers, had disobeyed orders and that such drastic measures had to be taken to bring them back under the authority of the agent.

Lone Man and other agency policemen had been warned several times by the dancers that if the police tried to interfere, they would regret it. The dancers were protected by *ogle wakan*—medicine shirts that were bulletproof. The night before the arrest, the Indian policemen were apprehensive. The role they were playing was an unnatural one—Sioux setting out to arrest another Sioux in the name of the white man. The policemen were certain, too, that their mission could not be accomplished without a fight. This might result in the worst crime a Sioux could commit—the killing of a fellow tribesman.

After Chaska had finished reading the orders from McLaughlin, Bull Head explained how the group would arrest Sitting Bull. First, they would move to Gray Eagle's cabin, a short distance east of Bull Head's. They would wait there, and just before dawn, they would quickly take up a position south of the river across from Sitting Bull's camp. The chief always had scouts out watching the road to the agency. Bull Head hoped the camp could be taken by surprise if he led his men in from the opposite direction. At dawn they would cross the river. The policemen would surround the chief's cabin, and the officers would enter to make the arrest.

Bull Head turned to Lone Man and said, "You used to belong to Sitting Bull's band and were always on the good side of the chief. I wish you would use your influence to keep order among the leaders who are going to become hostile."

Carignan knew that one of the details of McLaughlin's original plan had been that the police should take along a light spring wagon in which to whisk Sitting Bull away before his warriors realized what had happened. He reminded Bull Head of this now and warned him he couldn't take such a vehicle over the rough trail they would be using on the south side of the river.

Bull Head replied that he would not use a wagon. He had another plan. Sitting Bull had a favorite horse. It was an old gray circus animal, taught to perform tricks, that Buffalo Bill Cody had given to Sitting Bull when the chief left Cody's Wild West Show. Bull Head had decided that while he and the other officers were inside Sitting Bull's cabin, Red Bear and White Bird were to saddle the old gray and have it ready.

After the police had left, Carignan remained at Bull Head's cabin, sipping hot coffee before starting on the long, cold ride to the agency in his buggy.

At Gray Eagle's house, Bull Head and the rest of the police passed away the uneasy hours before dawn by telling old war stories. While they sat thus, ten more policemen rode in from Oak Creek. At last it was time to go. The Indians knelt before a crucifix and prayed to the white man's God, wondering while their lips formed the words whether, perhaps, the dancers' Ghost Shirts really were bulletproof.

The prayers finished, the policemen went outside, mounted their horses, and started for the river in double file.

The mood of the men was somber. A freezing drizzle had begun to add physical discomfort to their apprehension. "As we went through the Grand River bottoms," Lone Man recalled, "it seemed as if the owls were hooting at us. The coyotes were howling all around us, too, and someone remarked that the owls and the coyotes were giving us warning—so beware, he said."

At 5:30 A.M., when it was just barely light enough to see, the police crossed the river behind Sitting Bull's cabin. Fanning out, they galloped into the village of about twenty lodges. The dogs gave instant alarm. The policemen dismounted and swiftly surrounded Sitting Bull's cabin.

Inside, the great Hunkpapa chief was struggling to awaken. The noise of pounding hooves and barking dogs had interrupted his sound sleep. There was the thud of a rifle butt against his door, and it flew open. Beside him his wife gave a soft cry. Instantly the small cabin was full of shadowy figures. One of them struck a match and lighted the kerosene lamp on its wall bracket. The cabin's humble furnishings and its startled occupants were suddenly visible. White canvas stretched halfway up the chinked walls of the cabin. A stove stood in the middle of the long room. Strewn about the floor were the sleeping robes of Sitting Bull and his elder wife. It was a double cabin and now low murmurs could be heard from next door, where Sitting Bull's younger wife and his seventeen-year-old son, Crow Foot, slept.

Sitting Bull sat up and was immediately grabbed and dragged naked from his bed. Weasel Bear held the chief's right arm, and Eagle Man held his left. Lieutenant Bull Head laid his hand on the chief's shoulder and said, "You are under arrest. I have come to take you to the agency."

Red Tomahawk threw his arms around the naked chief from behind and warned, "If you fight, you will be killed right here."

The chief replied quietly, "Let me put my clothes on, and I'll go with you."

As his wife handed his clothing to Sitting Bull, she said scornfully, "What are all of you jealous people doing here?"

It was impossible for Sitting Bull to dress, held as he was by three men. Weasel Bear snatched up a moccasin and thrust it out at the chief. The woman laughed contemptuously. "That is mine," she said.

One policeman began to pull on Sitting Bull's leggings. Another forced a moccasin on his foot. The chief protested, "I can dress myself." But they would not let him. Sitting Bull began to grow indignant at such insulting treatment.

Crow Foot entered the cabin. His father told him to go and saddle a horse. Bull Head informed him there was no need. It had already been taken care of. As the officers and their prisoner started through the door, the elder wife burst into a loud cry, the custom of Indian women when saying goodbye.

By now Sitting Bull had turned balky, angered by the way he was being treated when he had assured his captors that he would go peaceably. As the policemen tried to drag the chief through the doorway, he spread out his arms and legs. Eagle Man kicked Sitting Bull's legs aside, and they pushed him out the door, still only half dressed.

Alerted by the dogs and the cry of Sitting Bull's wife, the entire camp had roused and was crowding around the cabin. The leaders were complaining about the actions of the police. It was difficult for the police to hold them back. The police formed a cordon around the chief, but Sitting Bull's followers pressed tightly against them, shouting threats and insults. Some of the newly recruited police grew frightened.

The gray horse had not yet been brought around, and Sitting Bull and his captors had to wait, standing in front of the cabin doorway. Catch-the-Bear pushed his way to the front of the crowd, raging like a wounded grizzly. He would not permit Bull Head, whom he hated because of past humiliations, to carry off his beloved chief. "You think you are going to take him," he shouted to Bull Head. "You shall not do it." Turning to the mob, he cried, "Come now, let us protect our chief."

Some of the warriors began to press closer. The police staggered and stumbled as they attempted to keep their line from being broken.

Crow Foot came out of the cabin and surveyed the scene. He had never expected to see anything like it. He had been preparing for the chieftainship all his life, never playing with the other boys. "He grew old too early," said one who knew him.

Disillusioned by what he saw, Crow Foot said sadly to his father, "I had always thought you a brave chief. Now you allow yourself to be taken by the ceska maza [metal breasts]."

Shame was added by his son to the anger Sitting Bull felt. He knew his people had only been awaiting his command to fall upon the ceska maza. "I shall not go," he announced firmly.

By this time Sitting Bull's followers were pressing as

hard as they could to get close to their chief and protect him. The police tried to keep them back, begging them not to cause any trouble, but they would not listen.

"You shall not take our chief!" they screamed.

Catch-the-Bear, in the heat of the excitement, pulled his rifle out from beneath his blanket and fired at Bull Head. The police lieutenant, hit in the leg, fell backward. Turning as he fell, he fired his revolver upward toward Sitting Bull. The bullet struck the chief in the chest. At almost the same moment, Red Tomahawk fired from behind into the back of Sitting Bull's head. The mighty chief of the Hunkpapas was killed instantly.

Lone Man, seeing Bull Head, one of his dearest relatives, shot, sprang toward Catch-the-Bear, who again pulled the trigger of his Winchester. The hammer snapped harmlessly. Lone Man wrestled the rifle from the other's grasp, clubbed him with it, and shot him dead.

Enraged by the killing of their chief, Sitting Bull's people threw themselves upon the police with guns, clubs, and knives in a frenzy of hand-to-hand fighting. Bull Head was struck by three more bullets. Sergeant Shave Head was shot by one of Sitting Bull's headmen. Four more policemen went down. Several of Sitting Bull's followers dropped, wounded or dead.

Just a moment before Sitting Bull announced that he would not go, his horse had been brought around. With the air filled with shouts and gunshots, the old gray horse must have imagined himself back in Buffalo Bill's Wild West Show. In the midst of the bloody struggle, he sat down, raised his hoof, and began performing the whole repertoire of tricks he had been taught during his circus days. No bullet touched him.

The macabre sight struck terror into the hearts of some of the policemen. Had the spirit of the mighty Sitting Bull entered the horse's body? they wondered.

While the old horse went gravely through his circus routine, most of the police took cover behind Sitting Bull's cabin, for most of the chief's followers had made a dash for the timber along the riverbank and were firing from there.

Second Sergeant Red Tomahawk, in command now that his lieutenant and first sergeant were wounded, ordered some of the police to carry Bull Head into the cabin and make him as comfortable as possible. The lieutenant had been shot in the right arm, the right knee, and through the body. While gathering up blankets in the cabin to make a bed for Bull Head, one of the policemen found Crow Foot hiding in a corner behind the canvas sheeting. Upon being discovered, he pleaded, "You have killed my father. Do not kill me. I wish to live!"

The police asked their mortally wounded lieutenant what to do. Bull Head's reply was bitter. "Kill him. They have killed me."

Red Tomahawk struck the boy a blow that sent him sprawling through the door. As Crow Foot lay dazed on the ground outside, two more policemen, with tears streaming down their faces, shot him.

Red Tomahawk, wasting no more time, ordered Hawk Man to ride as fast as he could and bring the soldiers. Hawk Man, apparently unawed by the circus horse, mounted the old gray and galloped off toward Oak Creek.

Hawk Man discovered the troops only three miles north of Grand River. Colonel Drum and Captain E. G. Fechet had decided that instead of halting at Oak Creek as originally planned, the captain should take his cavalry squadron ten or twelve miles closer to Grand River in order to be nearer to Sitting Bull's camp in case of trouble. The squadron was accompanied by two mounted, rapid-fire guns— a Hotchkiss gun and a Gatling gun.

The excited Hawk Man told Captain Fechet that all the police had been killed and that he was the only one who had escaped. The captain hastily penned a note to Colonel Drum repeating Hawk Man's report and stating that he and his squadron were rushing to the relief of any policemen who might still be alive. After dispatching Hawk Man to the agency with this message, Fechet formed his men into columns and started off.

Almost at once they were met by a second messenger from Red Tomahawk, who gave a more accurate report. He informed the captain that the police were pinned down in Sitting Bull's cabin, nearly out of ammunition, and could not hold out much longer. The captain ordered his columns into a gallop.

Pressing up the last ridge before reaching the Grand River Valley, the Hotchkiss gun hit a rut and flipped over. The harness broke, and the mule ran off. The ambulance, coming up behind, halted, and Hospital Steward August Nickel leaped out. A brawny man of enormous strength, Nickel crawled into the back of the ambulance, braced his feet against the tailgate, and gripped the shafts of the gun carriage. The ambulance driver cracked his whip, and the vehicle moved up the slope. The muscles in Nickel's thick arms took the strain, and the Hotchkiss gun followed.

By the time the rest of the group reached the crest of the ridge, Captain Fechet had surveyed the valley. Below and immediately in front of him lay the Hunkpapa settlement. From a knoll to his right, Indians were firing at Sitting Bull's cabin. Shots were coming from the timber along the river and from the cabin itself. Fechet could not be certain where the Indian policemen were. To find out, he raised a white flag, a signal that had been arranged with the police beforehand. No white flag was flown in response. Thinking perhaps the hostiles had taken over the cabin, Fechet ordered the Hotchkiss gun into place and had a round fired into the open space between the cabin and the timber.

Inside the cabin, the police searched wildly for something that would serve as a white flag. Lone Man ripped a piece of sheeting from the wall, tied it to a stick, and dashed outside waving it.

Knowing now that the police still held Sitting Bull's house, Fechet had Lieutenants Slocum and Steele, with their men

dismounted, advance directly on the house. Lieutenant
Crowder, with G Troop, was ordered to move along the
crest and protect the right flank of this dismounted line.
Fechet had the Hotchkiss gun open fire on the timber and
on the party of Indians firing from the knoll on his right.
As Slocum's line approached the house, the police came out
and joined it. The fire from the mounted gun had sent the
Hunkpapas fleeing from the timber. They scattered into
the hills on the south side of the river. Slocum's line pushed
into the timber, flushing out the few Indians who remained.
These crossed the river and joined their fellow tribesmen
in the hills. The troops pursued them but could not catch
them.

Fechet then ordered the dismounted line to fall back
to the vicinity of the cabin and left pickets stationed at the
farthest points gained by the line.

Captain Fechet could never afterward put the scene out
of his mind. "I saw evidence of a most desperate encounter,"
he wrote later.

> In front of the house, and within a radius of fifty yards, were
> the bodies of 8 dead Indians, including that of Sitting Bull, and
> 2 dead horses. In the house were 4 dead policemen and 3
> wounded, 2 mortally. To add to the horror of the scene the
> squaws of Sitting Bull, who were in a small house nearby, kept up
> a great wailing.

In the cabin, Bull Head, knowing he was dying, asked
his friend Weasel Bear to look after his family. "Never let
them forget that I am the one who killed Sitting Bull," he
said. A few minutes later, when Turning Hawk came in to
see him, Bull Head again spoke proudly of his deed: "Sitting
Bull is dead and I killed him."

Red Tomahawk, who had shot Sitting Bull immediately
after the chief was struck by the charge from Bull Head's
revolver, also wanted to be remembered as the man who

Big Foot's Band, August 9, 1890

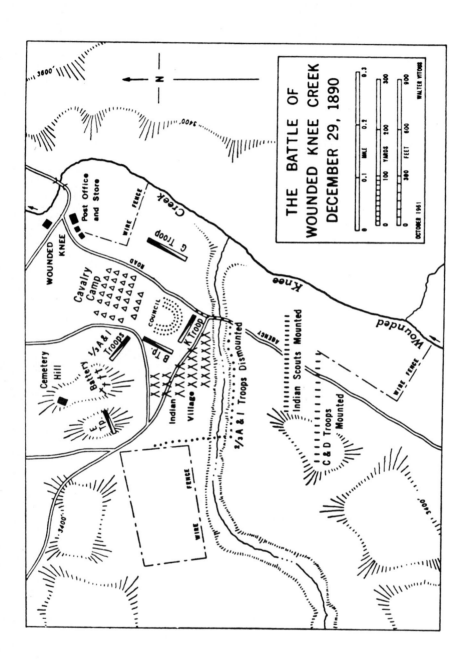

THE BATTLE OF
WOUNDED KNEE CREEK
DECEMBER 29, 1890

OCTOBER 1961   WALTER YETORS

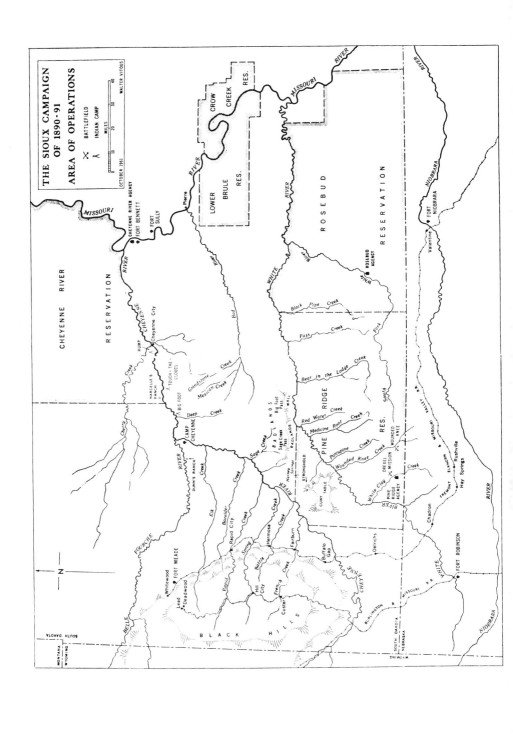

THE SIOUX CAMPAIGN
OF 1890-91
AREA OF OPERATIONS

✕ BATTLEFIELD
⅄ INDIAN CAMP

MILES
0 10 20 30 40

OCTOBER 1961   WALTER VITOUS

Short Bull

Kicking Bear

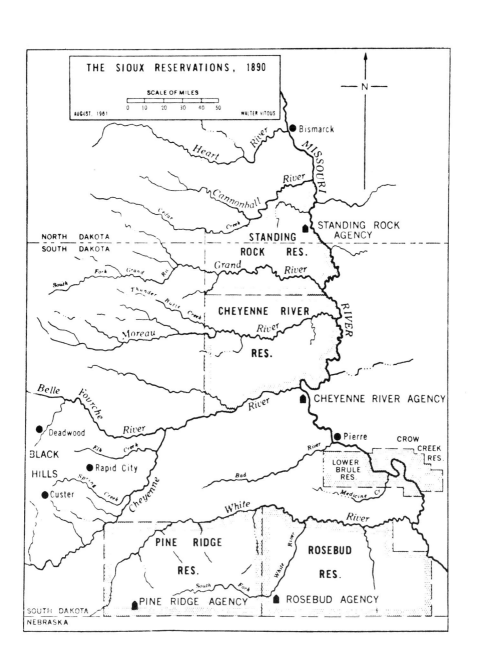

THE SIOUX RESERVATIONS, 1890

SCALE OF MILES

0   10   20   30   40   50

AUGUST, 1961   WALTER VITOUS

N

Bismarck

Heart   River

Cannonball   River

MISSOURI

Cedar   Creek

STANDING ROCK AGENCY

NORTH   DAKOTA

STANDING

SOUTH   DAKOTA

ROCK   RES.

South   Fork   Grand   R.   Grand   River

Thunder   Butte   Creek

CHEYENNE   RIVER

Moreau   River

RES.

RIVER

Belle   Fourche

River   CHEYENNE RIVER AGENCY

Deadwood

Elk   Creek

Pierre   CROW

BLACK   River   CREEK

HILLS   Rapid City   Spring   Creek   LOWER   RES.

Cheyenne   Bad   BRULE

Custer   RES.

Medicine   Cr.

White

River

PINE   RIDGE   ROSEBUD

White   River

RES.   RES.

South   Fork

PINE RIDGE AGENCY   ROSEBUD AGENCY

SOUTH   DAKOTA

NEBRASKA

Sitting Bull

Buffalo Bill Cody and General Miles near Pine Ridge, January 16, 1891

Big Foot

killed the great Hunkpapa chief. The army surgeon's report later stated either of the shots would have proved fatal.

Soon after the arrival of the troops, some of Policeman Strong Arm's family came to see what the fate of their relative had been. When they found his body lying in the stable, where he had been shot, they set up a great wailing. The rage of one of the kinsmen, Holy Medicine, focused on Sitting Bull, whose followers had killed Strong Arm. He picked up a neck-yoke lying in the stable, rushed over to the body of the dead chief, and beat the corpse savagely about the head and face. Holy Medicine was stopped by the soldiers. Sergeant James Hanaghan, to prevent further mutilation of the corpse, detailed Private A. L. Bloomer to stand guard over the body. Bloomer, fearing that the body would freeze to the ground, dragged it out of the pool of blood in which it lay.

Holy Medicine was not the only Sioux who was bitter because of the fact that Sitting Bull's followers had killed a relative. One of the policemen, grieving over a brother lying dead on the ground, burst into the smaller of Sitting Bull's cabins, intent on vengeance of some sort. He spied a full-length oil portrait of Sitting Bull hanging on the wall. He pulled it down, ripped the canvas with his rifle, and smashed the frame.

Fechet's squadron had been ordered to march that morning before they had had time to feed their horses and breakfast themselves. After making sure that there were no snipers left in the area, the soldiers built fires and tended their horses while breakfast was prepared. Captain Fechet had just raised a cup of coffee to his lips when an alarm was sounded. A lone Indian burst from the timber about eighty yards away. Riding a black horse, wearing a red Ghost Shirt, and carrying a feathered lance, he raced toward the soldiers, singing a Ghost Song.

Father, I thought you said
We were all going to live!

It was Crow Woman, one of the most fanatical of the dancers, who had set out to prove to his fellow tribesmen watching from the hills across the river that a Ghost Shirt would protect the wearer from white men's bullets.

The Indian police had given the alarm, and they opened fire. The rider wheeled and rode back into the timber only to reappear a moment later about four hundred yards up the valley. Again the fire of the police drove him back into the trees. He emerged a third time, this time galloping between two cavalrymen serving as pickets. They shot at him as he dashed past, but he escaped untouched up the valley. For many of the Hunkpapas, this was convincing proof of the magical qualities of the sacred garment.

Three hundred and thirty-three Hunkpapas had fled Standing Rock Reservation when the soldiers arrived. Half of them were not involved in the fracas around Sitting Bull's cabin. They were sleeping in their own cabins up and down the river while the bloody affair was taking place. But the word spread quickly, and, frightened by the killing of their chief and the arrival of the bluecoats, they left their homes and took to the hills. Captain Fechet was uncertain as to what to do about them. His orders had concerned the arrest of Sitting Bull and had said nothing about the chief's followers. Believing that pursuit might provoke the friendlies, through fear or anger, to join the dancers, Fechet wisely decided not to try to round up the Indians. He released Sitting Bull's widows and told them to get word to the people that the troops were leaving for Fort Yates and the Indians could return to their homes in safety. He also sent runners out with the message that any Indians who wished to come into the agency could join the troops. This move elicited a good response. Many of the friendlies, anxious to avoid more trouble, fell in with the cavalry columns as they made their way back to the fort.

The three wounded policemen, Bull Head, Shave Head, and Middle, were placed in the ambulance for the ride back to Fort Yates. There was some dispute about how the dead were to be carried back. There was only one wagon, and the policemen objected to their dead's sharing it with Sitting Bull's body. Only Red Tomahawk's stern order made them agree to the arrangement. They put the chief's body into the wagon first and then laid their own dead on top.

The bodies of the seven followers of Sitting Bull who had died fighting for their chief were dragged into the stable and left there. They were buried later in a common grave by a Congregational missionary, T. L. Riggs, who arrived with some Christian Indians after the battle.

As the troops started back to the agency, Lone Man and Afraid-of-Hawk, after a last look at their dead friends and relatives, started home.

As Lone Man approached his cabin, he called out to his family to prepare a sweat bath for him. He felt he had to purify himself after the bloody fight with his fellow tribesmen before going into the presence of his family. After his bath, clean clothes were brought to him, and he burned those he had worn during the fight. Only then would he enter his cabin for a reunion with his family.

The next day he took his wife and children into the agency and reported to McLaughlin. The agent laid his hand on Lone Man's shoulder and said, "I feel proud of you for the very brave way you have carried out your part in the fight against the Ghost Dancers."

Lone Man later recalled, "I was not very brave right at that moment. His words nearly set me crying."

That same day, the soldier who taught the small school at Fort Yates dismissed his pupils at noon and gave them the rest of the day off. A runner had arrived with the news that Captain Fechet and his troops were bringing in the body of Sitting Bull. It was a special day, a holiday. No one wanted to miss seeing the army bring in the famous Sioux chief.

About the middle of the afternoon, the cavalcade arrived. The wagon carrying the chief's body came first, followed by the ambulance. Both vehicles were escorted by the surviving Indian policemen and the friendlies who were coming into the agency. Many of the women were singing death songs. The cavalry was nearly a mile behind, and the infantry was even farther to the rear. The wagons passed through the fort and continued into the agency. The cavalry halted at the post stables.

The bodies of the dead policemen were placed in the agency meeting hall, after which the wagon returned to the fort and deposited the body of Sitting Bull in the charnel house behind the post hospital.

In the boarding school, which also housed a tiny hospital run by Catholic sisters, agency and army doctors did what they could for the three wounded policemen. Bull Head and Shave Head could not be saved. They could merely be made as comfortable as possible.

Shave Head, knowing he had only hours to live, asked McLaughlin, "Did I do well?" The agent nodded, unable to speak. "Then," said Shave Head, "I wish to die in the white man's faith, to which my five children belong. Send for my wife so that we can be married by the Black Robe before I die."

McLaughlin sent a man to Shave Head's cabin, eighteen miles away, to bring in the Indian's wife. Fifteen minutes before she arrived, Shave Head died in the arms of Father Bernard Strassmaier. The policeman's wife sang the death song over his body.

Bull Head died the next day. The third injured policeman, Middle, recovered from his wounds.

A funeral was held for the six slain policemen on the afternoon of December 17. The small frame church of Congregational missionary George W. Reed was jammed with Standing Rock Indians. After the joint services by the Reverend Reed and Father Strassmaier, the bodies were taken to the cemetery near the Catholic mission church. A company of infantry fired three volleys over the graves, and the sad notes of "Taps" sounded over the mourning wails of the Sioux.

Sitting Bull was buried without ceremony. He was so hated by the mourners of the dead policemen that they would not consent to the Hunkpapa chief's being buried in the same cemetery as their own dead. A grave was dug for Sitting Bull in a corner of the post cemetery at Fort Yates, and his burial took place quietly. So bitter was the feeling against Sitting Bull that, as Father Strassmaier later said, "It was deemed unwise to give the chief a public funeral."

Private J. F. Waggoner, detailed for work in the carpentry shop, made a simple wooden casket to hold Sitting Bull's body. While he was building it, soldiers kept coming in for the honor of driving a nail into the chief's coffin. Waggoner, who had known Sitting Bull well, disapproved. He had the same respect and admiration for the great Hunkpapa warrior as he had for any good army officer. "For he was surely a fighter, a thinker, a chief, and a gentleman. He had eaten many a meal in my house, and I cannot but speak well of Sitting Bull," he later declared.

When the box was finished, Private Waggoner took it to the charnel house; Sitting Bull's body was placed in it, wrapped in a blanket frozen stiff with blood. The rough coffin was loaded onto a two-wheeled cart and drawn down the slope to the post cemetery by an old army mule named Caesar. Accompanying the coffin were Waggoner; Saddler, a hospital steward; Johnny Hughes, a teamster; Lieutenant P. G. Wood of the Twelfth Infantry; and his son, Guy.

It was midafternoon. The grave had already been dug. Before the coffin was lowered into the hole, its lid was raised. Five gallons of chloride of lime were poured into it, and on top of that a large amount of muriatic acid. The mixture produced thick fumes; the lid was hastily nailed down, and the box was lowered into the grave. Four military prisoners, assigned to the grave-digging detail, began to shovel dirt on top of the coffin. The smoke from the box continued to seep through the loose earth until the grave was nearly half filled with dirt.

Agent McLaughlin arrived about this time and stood watching with the others while the grave of his old adversary was filled in with earth.

In Private Waggoner's opinion, the manner in which the burial was handled was shoddy and disgraceful. He recalled, "We laid the noble old Chief away without a hymn or a prayer or a sprinkle of earth. Quicklime was used instead. It made me angry. I had always admired the Chief for his courage and his generalship. He was a *man!*"

Sitting Bull was also the last of the great Sioux chiefs to resist the loss of the old beloved ways and the adoption of the white man's culture. With Sitting Bull gone, there was no other Sioux of any stature to stand before his people as a symbol of the old way of life.

Years later, at the death of McLaughlin, the writer of the agent's obituary declared that the death of Sitting Bull "put a stop forever to the domination of the ancient regime among the Sioux of the Standing Rock Reservation." He was right.

7

The Search for Big Foot

THE KILLING of Sitting Bull had a shattering effect upon his people. Nearly four hundred of them fled in fear and anger southward toward the reservation line, without taking time to pack food or clothing or any other necessities. Hungry, cold, some of them wounded, they didn't stop in their breathless flight until they reached the Miniconjou settlements on the Moreau River, within the Cheyenne River Reservation.

McLaughlin realized the danger the Hunkpapas posed, given their state of mind, if they joined Short Bull and Kicking Bear on the Stronghold or the Miniconjous along the Cheyenne River. He immediately sent out messengers to intercept Sitting Bull's people and coax them to return to their own agency.

McLaughlin's emissaries caught up with the fugitives in the Miniconjou settlements. The Hunkpapas agreed to hold a council; there they listened to promises of the kind treatment that awaited them if they returned home. Their fears laid to rest, 160 of Sitting Bull's people started back toward their agency. Eighty-eight remained for a while longer; then they, too, returned to their homes. The rest, probably more infuriated over the killing of their great chief than afraid, started south again, heading for Big Foot's camp on the Cheyenne River.

Big Foot was revered among the Miniconjous just as Sitting Bull had been by the Hunkpapas. But the Miniconjou chief was respected as a gifted negotiator rather than as a great warrior. Few other chiefs in the history of the Miniconjous had possessed such skill in bringing quarreling factions together. Among the Sioux, Big Foot was known as a great compromiser. Unhappily, this was not the reputation that Big Foot enjoyed among government officials and the army. Big Foot had remained one of those chiefs who would not give up the old ways of life. When the Ghost Dance religion appeared among the Sioux, he embraced it wholeheartedly, excited about the prospect of the world's returning to the state it had been in before the white man came. Big Foot took his people to join Hump's band on Cherry Creek, where the two groups threw themselves into an orgy of dancing.

After Hump had been persuaded by his old friend Captain Ezra Ewers to give up the dance and return to the agency and his old job as chief of police, Big Foot grew disheartened. He abandoned the dance camp and led his people back to their cluster of cabins below the fork of the Cheyenne River. Thereafter, he took no part in the dance, although some of his people continued it, urged onward by Yellow Bird, a medicine man.

Despite Big Foot's change of heart, and because the fanatical Yellow Bird kept the Ghost Dance alive in Big Foot's band, the chief was considered by General Miles to be the biggest troublemaker among the Sioux now that Sitting Bull was dead. The general had not forgotten Big Foot's command to his people at the Cherry Creek dance camp on November 25 to gather all the guns and cartridges they could find, nor the reports received at that time that Big

Foot's dancers were spoiling for a fight. Miles wanted Big Foot arrested at the earliest opportunity.

Lieutenant Colonel Edwin V. Sumner was assigned to keep an eye on Big Foot. On December 3 he had assumed command of the "camp of observation" that had been established a few miles up the Cheyenne River from the chief's settlement. The command post was called Camp Cheyenne, and from it Sumner was also to protect the tiny white settlements and isolated ranches on the Belle Fourche and Cheyenne rivers. For this purpose he was given some infantry and cavalry totaling about two hundred men. No hint of Miles's intention to arrest Big Foot had yet filtered down to the colonel.

A cavalryman, Sumner had compiled a distinguished service record as an Indian fighter. During the many years he had fought the Indians, he had developed a profound respect and sympathy for the red man. Shortly after Sumner took command of Camp Cheyenne, Big Foot and some of his sub-chiefs paid him a visit and stayed for two days. The chief sensed the officer's sympathy.

"Without exception," Sumner informed General Miles, the chief and his headmen "seemed not only willing but anxious to obey my order to remain quietly at home, and particularly wished me to inform my superiors that they were all on the side of the government in the trouble" plaguing the reservations.

Colonel Sumner returned the chief's social call, and during the next two weeks, the two men visited each other frequently. Although Sumner was convinced that Big Foot's friendliness was genuine, he observed that many members of the band did not share the chief's attitude. Yet he reported that he was "impressed with the idea that Big Foot was making an extraordinary effort to keep his followers quiet." Sumner expected no trouble.

The killing of Sitting Bull appeared to have no effect upon the friendlies at Pine Ridge or the hostiles on the Stronghold. The only activity in that area was the tiny war being waged between the hostiles and the cowboy army commanded by Colonel H. M. Day. When the settlers around Pine Ridge grew impatient with General Brooke for not forcing a fight with the rebels on the Stronghold, Day formed the so-called South Dakota Militia, made up of sixty-two ranchers and cowboys. On Sunday, December 14, the day before Sitting Bull was killed, Day's militia fought four skirmishes with parties of Indians. Eighteen of the ragtag army crossed the Cheyenne River on December 15 and rode toward the Stronghold. The dancers launched an attack and drove the militia back across the river. In another skirmish at Phinney's Ranch, between Spring and Battle creeks, Day and ten of his cowboys held off a party of Sioux for four hours. Finally, the Indians set fire to the corral and, while the cowboys fought the fire there, ignited the prairie, too. Only a shift in the wind saved the cowboys, and the Indians withdrew.

Brooke was at that time trying to persuade General Miles to authorize a double-pronged assault on the Stronghold, one force to attack from the south, the other from the north. Miles was not receptive to the idea, and Brooke decided to try another peace offensive. He hoped to repeat the success Louis Shangreau and his party had had in convincing so many of the dancers to leave the Stronghold. What a small party had done, perhaps a large party could do even better. This time Brooke planned to send five hundred friendlies to the Stronghold to try to negotiate with their rebel kinsmen. Miles liked this plan, and, fearing that Colonel Day's cowboy militia might touch off a fight at the wrong moment, he ordered Day to keep his troops north of the Cheyenne River.

The week before Sitting Bull was killed, runners from the friendly chiefs on Pine Ridge arrived at Big Foot's settlement. The Oglala headmen were offering the skillful negotiator one hundred ponies to come to Pine Ridge and restore peace on the agency. Although his sub-chiefs urged him to accept the offer, Big Foot was undecided. At last he said that he would wait and take his people into his own agency on December 22 for the regular issue of their rations. Upon his return home, he would decide whether or not to go to Pine Ridge.

On the very day Sitting Bull was killed, Big Foot, unaware of the tragedy that was taking place around Sitting Bull's cabin, started eastward with his people toward their agency. Colonel Sumner had been happy with Big Foot's decision. He believed that the influence of Hump, who had forsaken the dance, and the sight of the bluecoats around Fort Bennett might calm some of the more zealous dancers in Big Foot's band. Two days later Sumner was wishing that Big Foot had stayed at home.

On December 17 Sumner received a telegram that had been sent the day before from headquarters in St. Paul. It was not a direct order, but it indicated that General Ruger desired Sumner to arrest Big Foot whenever Sumner felt it could be accomplished with a minimum of trouble. It was the first indication Sumner had been given that his superiors thought it necessary to arrest the Miniconjou chief. The telegram took Sumner by surprise, and, to make matters worse, Big Foot was gone and no longer under Sumner's direct observation—a fact that he was certain would vex General Ruger.

More disturbing news arrived later in the day. Scouts from downriver reported that the Hunkpapas sent stampeding by the killing of Sitting Bull were heading southward toward Cheyenne River to incite the Miniconjous to join them in a dash to Pine Ridge. What they planned to do upon reaching the agency no one knew, but with the news they carried, and in their distraught emotional condition, they could touch off an explosion.

Uncertain as to what he should do, Sumner weighed the situation for a day. Then, on the morning of December 19, he sent a platoon of twenty-two cavalrymen, under Lieutenant R. J. Duff, toward Cherry Creek, where Big Foot now camped, to find out what they could about the state of affairs.

Big Foot had made his camp on Cherry Creek on the night of December 17, two days before Lieutenant Duff set off with his patrol. During that first night in camp, a runner had brought word to Big Foot that many soldiers were coming from the east. After the death of Sitting Bull, a message had been sent to Colonel H. C. Merriam, whose Seventh Infantry had been trying to cross the ice-choked Missouri River since December 7, and who now commanded all the troops in the vicinity. Merriam had been ordered to march up the Chey-enne River and to join forces with Sumner. Two companies had finally succeeded in crossing the Missouri, and it was news of these that the runner carried into Big Foot's camp. The next day two of Sitting Bull's people, one with a bullet in his leg, found Big Foot's camp and told of the death of Sitting Bull and the flight of his people southward out of their reser-vation toward Big Foot's settlement. The news frightened Big Foot's people, and the chief himself was no longer sure that he should continue on the journey to the agency when so many troops lay in that direction.

The next day, December 19, Big Foot took his people across the river, where the grass was better, and camped near Cavanaugh's store. James Cavanaugh and his two grown sons were frightened. They claimed later that many of the braves were painted for war and that the band was staging a Ghost Dance. When some of the warriors entered the store and said they were hungry, Cavanaugh took the hint. He gave them coffee, flour, and sugar. When the Indians also said they had no beef, Cavanaugh invited them to kill one of his calves. As soon as the Indians had left to round up the calf, Cavanaugh and his sons fled their store. They ran into Lieutenant Duff's patrol about ten miles east of Camp Cheyenne. The store-keeper claimed that Big Foot's men had robbed him and that a few of Sitting Bull's people had arrived in Big Foot's camp. Duff relayed this news back to Colonel Sumner, who im-mediately started for the scene with his entire command.

On the same day Big Foot moved his camp into Cav-anaugh's front yard, the chief also sent ten of his men to search for the refugees from Sitting Bull's village and offer them food and shelter in his own camp. The search party found the refugees camped at the mouth of Cherry Creek. They were a pitiful sight. Without lodging, food, and cooking utensils, and wearing only the clothing they had on when routed out of bed on the morning of Sitting Bull's death, the Hunkpapa women huddled, shivering, around a few fires. Many were singing death songs, mourning Sitting Bull and those who were killed with him. All of the men were across the river in Hump's village.

Big Foot's emissaries crossed the river and found the Hunkpapa refugees in council with Hump and his Miniconjou headmen. When the emissaries extended Big Foot's invitation to the refugees, Hump argued strenuously against their accepting it. He shouted: "You don't have to take them to Big Foot's camp. I will take all these people to the agency. You people want to fight, and I will bring some infantry to help you."

Hump motioned his warriors, weapons cocked, into a menacing circle around Big Foot's men. But the Sitting Bull refugees protested such belligerent action, warning Hump that if he meant to fight, they would be on the side of Big Foot's messengers. When the situation cooled, thirty-eight Hunkpapa refugees and thirty of Hump's own young warriors decided to join forces with Big Foot. One hundred sixty-six of the Hunkpapas remained with Hump and later surrendered to Colonel Merriam, who had at last managed to cross the Missouri and was marching up the Cheyenne. The Hunkpapas who surrendered were sent down the Missouri to Fort Sully, where they were held prisoners. Colonel Merriam set up temporary headquarters at Cheyenne City to await developments.

On the eve of December 20, Sumner and his troops, on their way toward Big Foot's temporary camp on Cherry Creek, reached Narcisse Narcelle's ranch on the north side of the Cheyenne. After spending the night there, the command set out upon the remaining twelve-mile journey to Big

Foot's camp. It appears that the Miniconjou chief had learned that Sumner was coming to see him, for after proceeding only a few miles downriver, the colonel was met by Big Foot, one of his headmen, and the two Hunkpapa refugees who had arrived at Big Foot's camp with the news of Sitting Bull's death.

Sumner scolded the chief for giving refuge to the runaway Hunkpapas. Big Foot replied with dignity that he could not have turned away kinsmen who came to him footsore, hungry, and nearly naked. Sumner softened his tone when he discovered that the two Hunkpapas with Big Foot "answered his description perfectly," but he told the chief that he would have to give up his trip to the agency for rations and take his people back home. Big Foot informed Sumner that he had already decided to do this. His people had heard that the troops under Colonel Merriam were coming toward them from the east, and they had been growing frightened.

Big Foot gathered his people together, and, escorted by Sumner's cavalry, the entire band turned about and headed back to their settlement. They numbered 333 men, women, and children, including 38 Hunkpapa refugees. The group camped for the night at Narcelle's ranch, completely surrounded by troops.

A feast provided by the soldiers that night seemed to dispel much of the uneasiness felt by the Indians, but when they resumed their journey the next morning, their good humor faded. Sumner had decided that, rather than dropping the Indians off at their own settlement, he would escort them to Camp Cheyenne, where he could keep an eye on them. The Indians did not like this decision, nor did they like the way Sumner organized the march. The Indians had a number of wagons with them. Sumner divided the wagons into two sections and loaded all those Indians without ponies—chiefly women, children, and old men—into the vehicles. Each section of wagons was escorted by a group of cavalry and moved off separately, with Big Foot riding in a wagon near the head of the column. The mounted warriors formed the third section of the march. Behind this caravan marched the infantry. The Indians resented being placed under such rigid control. After a few miles, Sumner noted that some of the young men had painted their faces and were making a great show of the rifles they carried as they broke away from their escort and rode up and down beside the two wagon sections.

A few miles from the Narcelle ranch, one of the wagons, passing through a gate, caught on a fence post. Its wheels locked, and the women, afraid the soldiers might be angered by this mishap, did their best to get the wagon through. In their fright, however, they only succeeded in tangling the horses in their harness. An officer rode up and ordered the women to quit blocking the gate. Infuriated by his tone, the warriors broke loose. Black Fox, son-in-law of Big Foot, pointed his rifle at the officer, who quickly retreated. The other warriors milled about on their ponies, and when the gate was finally cleared, they raced along the column, shouting and brandishing their rifles. The women, expecting a fight, began throwing their belongings out of the wagons, preparing to flee.

As the warriors drew near the head of the caravan, Lieutenant Duff ordered his advance guard to face to the rear and form a skirmish line. When the warriors found themselves confronting a line of carbines pointed directly at them, they wheeled and drifted back to the rear.

Sumner asked Big Foot to try to calm his followers, and the chief sent messengers up and down the columns assuring the people that the soldiers meant them no harm and that there would be no trouble if they would do as the soldiers asked.

Later, when they drew within sight of their own cabins, the Miniconjous once again became agitated. Their settlement must have looked like a haven of safety to them, and they would not continue.

Big Foot came to Sumner and said,

> I will go with you to your camp, but there will be trouble in trying to force these women and children, cold and hungry as they are, away from their homes. This is their home, where the

Government has ordered them to stay, and none of my people
have committed a single act requiring their removal by force.

The colonel recognized the wisdom of the chief's words.
Any attempt to force these people to continue toward Camp
Cheyenne would most certainly precipitate a fight. In a re-
port Sumner filed later, he explained,

> I concluded that one of two things must happen. I must either
> consent to their going into their village or bring on a fight; and,
> if the latter, must be the aggressor, and, if the aggressor, what
> possible reason could I produce for making an attack on peace-
> able, quiet Indians on their reservation and at their homes, kill-
> ing perhaps many of them and offering, without any justification,
> the lives of many officers and enlisted men.

Sumner consented to allow Big Foot's band to remain in
their settlement if the chief would promise to come to Camp
Cheyenne the next day for a council, bringing with him all
of the refugees from Sitting Bull's band. Big Foot gave his
promise, and the troops went on to Camp Cheyenne.

During the night a wire was delivered to Sumner from
General Miles, who had arrived in Rapid City to take personal command of all military units in Dakota. The wire informed Sumner that two hundred Indians were rumored to
be ranging through western North Dakota. Miles had received information that the Indians had a troop of cavalry
surrounded. Miles discounted the rumors, and he was correct
in doing so—later evidence proved them false. Nevertheless,
he wanted Sumner to lead a company to the northern edge
of the Black Hills in case the rumors turned out to be true.
Immediately upon his return to Camp Cheyenne, Sumner
had sent a wire to the general explaining his decision not to
bring Big Foot in. However, the wire had not yet arrived.
Miles, believing Sumner to be bringing in Big Foot and his
band, directed the colonel to bring the prisoners to Fort
Meade as rapidly as possible. "Be careful they do not escape,"
he warned, "and look out for other Indians."

Early on the morning of December 23, Sumner sent another wire to General Miles and declared that if Big Foot did not come to the camp as he had promised, Sumner would send the cavalry to bring him in. He then dispatched scouts to Big Foot's camp.

The hours passed. At noon Big Foot had not shown up, and there was no word from the scouts. Sumner ordered dinner brought to his tent and considered his choices. He could go out after Big Foot and arrest him as Miles wished. If the story about the two hundred hostiles sweeping down from the north was true, Sumner would have his hands full dealing with them. It would be a nuisance to try to keep Big Foot under surveillance at the same time. But arresting Big Foot would infuriate the chief's warriors. Even if they did not succeed in preventing the arrest, the braves would scatter and pose an ever-present and elusive threat to Sumner.

Besides, Sumner could not agree with the assessment of Big Foot made weeks ago by authorities who were far from the scene. Sumner was convinced that Big Foot, far from being the agitator the officials thought, was the main restraining force upon his warriors. To remove his peaceful influence at this time seemed unwise.

The other choice seemed much more sensible and less likely to precipitate serious trouble. Sumner concluded that Big Foot must be persuaded to go to his agency. There he would be under the observation of the garrison at Fort Bennett. But would the chief and his people go? Word that Colonel Merriam's troops were moving up the river had turned them back once. Would they agree to start the journey again?

Sumner had just finished eating when a visitor was shown into his tent. He was John Dunn, a rancher who lived on the Belle Fourche River a few miles from Camp Cheyenne. The man had come to sell fresh eggs and butter to the colonel, but it suddenly struck Sumner that Dunn possessed something much more important at the moment than fresh eggs and butter—a knowledge of and friendship with Big Foot

that had developed over the ten years Dunn had been ranch-
ing in the area. He was known to the Indians as Red Beard.
Sumner asked Dunn to go to Big Foot and try to persuade
the chief to lead his people to their agency. Dunn didn't
want the job and said so, but Sumner persisted until finally
the rancher agreed. The colonel sent Felix Benoit, an interpreter, with Dunn. As soon as the two men had ridden away,
Sumner had "Boots and Saddles" sounded, and in a short
while, he led his command down the valley toward Big Foot's
village.

On the outskirts of the Miniconjou settlement, Benoit and
Dunn met the two scouts Sumner had sent out early that
morning. The interpreter stopped to talk with them, while
Dunn went on into the village. Benoit asked the scouts why
Big Foot had not come into Camp Cheyenne that morning as
he had promised. The scouts replied that the Sitting Bull
refugees had run away rather than accompany Big Foot to
Camp Cheyenne, and the chief had been afraid to come in
without them. The three men then went into the village and
found Dunn and Big Foot talking in front of the chief's cabin,
surrounded by a restless, excited crowd.

"I am ordered to go down to Bennett tomorrow morning,"
Big Foot shouted to his people. "We must all go to Bennett;
if we don't, John Dunn is sent here to tell me that the soldiers
will come here in the morning and make us go, and shoot us
if they have to." Catching sight of Benoit, Big Foot asked
him if Dunn was telling the truth. Benoit replied that he was.

It was not true, of course, and why the two white men
added the threat to Summer's message remains a mystery.
Perhaps they believed a threat would carry more weight
than persuasion and be more likely to produce results. But
the threat only produced increased anger and confusion
among warriors who were already hostile and uneasy.

When Dunn, Benoit, and the two scouts had left, Big Foot
called a council. The chief declared that he believed their
best move was to do nothing, to remain in their settlement

and await developments. But many of his headmen did not
agree. They reminded Big Foot of the troops marching at
them from two directions—Sumner's from the west, and Merriam's from the east. Some of the sub-chiefs voiced their
conviction that they should go into their agency as Sumner
wanted them to. Others argued that Big Foot should accept
the invitation from the Oglala chiefs to go to Pine Ridge
and restore peace there.

A compromise was finally reached. They would move up
Deep Creek, hide in the hills, and watch from there to see if
the bluecoats really were coming.

Benoit, glancing back at the village before he, Dunn, and
the two scouts moved out of sight, noticed an unusual amount
of activity. Ponies were being rounded up, and wagons were
being loaded. He called Dunn's attention to the preparations,
and they assumed the Indians had decided to leave for the
agency immediately. Sending one of the scouts back to find
out for sure what was going on, the two white men continued
up the river. They found Sumner camped about five miles
from the village and reported to him. Not long afterward,
the scout returned and said that the women and children
were very frightened, and it did indeed appear that the
whole village was preparing to leave for the Cheyenne
Agency immediately. It was now late afternoon, and Sumner
sent three scouts to Big Foot to tell the chief not to leave
until morning.

One of the scouts returned quickly with the news that the
Indians had already left, but instead of heading east toward
the agency, they had started south. This was disturbing news
to Sumner. To the south lay the Pine Ridge Agency, and
from the beginning of the present crisis, the army had been
determined to prevent Sioux on the other reservations from
joining the rebels on the Stronghold. It was Sumner's hope
that Big Foot was merely going south to take the ridge road
to his agency, hoping to avoid Merriam's troops, which were
moving up the valley road. Sumner sent out more scouts.

If Big Foot turned east when his party reached the ridge road, Sumner could relax. If the chief continued on south, he would have to be stopped.

Colonel Sumner was not the only one with a problem. Big Foot had one, too. That night in the hills above Deep Creek, he and his sub-chiefs held another council. All the headmen urged Big Foot to go to Pine Ridge and there make the peace for which he'd been promised 100 ponies. Big Foot argued that he could not go. Not only had he given his word to Sumner that he would not go to Pine Ridge, but he did not feel well and did not feel up to making the long journey south. He would like to stay home, but as long as they had to leave, he preferred to go to the Cheyenne Agency.

His headmen, however, feared a trap. Fort Bennett was too close to the agency for comfort. Who could tell what the soldiers would do to them when they arrived there? They insisted that Big Foot go to Pine Ridge, and at last he yielded. He sent a message to the colonel by one of Sumner's scouts explaining his situation.

The message was delivered to Sumner the next morning. It was the day before Christmas. Still worried about the rumors of hostiles to the north, Sumner did not follow Big Foot's trail. Instead, he returned to Camp Cheyenne. A few hours later, a courier arrived from Fort Meade with the following telegram from General Miles:

Rapid City, [December] 23d.

To Colonel E. V. Sumner,
Commanding Cheyenne:
    (Through Commanding Officer Fort Meade)
    Report about hostile Indians near Little Missouri not believed. The attitude of Big Foot has been defiant and hostile, and you are authorized to arrest him or any of his people and to take them to Meade or Bennett. There are some 30 young warriors that run [sic] away from Hump's camp without authority, and if an opportunity is given they will undoubtedly join those in the Bad Lands. The Standing Rock Indians also have no right to be there and they should be arrested. The division commander directs,

therefore, that you secure Big Foot and the 20 [*sic*] Cheyenne River Indians, and the Standing Rock Indians, and if necessary round up the whole camp and disarm them, and take them to Fort Meade or Bennett.

.   .   .   .   .

By command of General Miles.

Maus,
Captain and Aide-de-Camp

Sumner now had the unenviable job of informing the general that Big Foot had slipped away from him. Miles was so furious that he immediately began an investigation in order to bring Sumner before a court of inquiry. Sumner was saved only by the fact that he received no *direct* orders to arrest Big Foot until the general's telegram arrived on December 24. It was then too late, for Big Foot was gone.

The best hope of intercepting Big Foot lay with Colonel Eugene A. Carr's Sixth Cavalry, whose three squadrons were ranging east and west from the base camp located at the spot where Rapid Creek emptied into the Cheyenne River— about twenty miles north of the Stronghold. Colonel Sumner sent a message alerting Carr that Big Foot was headed south. If Carr moved swiftly to the east, he might be able to intercept the Miniconjous.

Only four troops of the Sixth Cavalry were in camp, but within hours, they were heading eastward with two Hotchkiss guns. By evening they had reached the northern edge of that awesome and intimidating area of the country called the South Dakota Badlands. It was Christmas Eve.

"The night was very cold," recalled one of the officers,

and the alkaline pools in the vicinity were frozen solid. Those who had brought any food divided with the others as far as possible, but Christmas morning dawned upon a lot of half-frozen, uncomfortable men who had spent a cheerless night, alternately heaping wood on the fires and then trying to sleep on saddle blankets.

Two of the troops that had been away from the Sixth Cavalry base camp when Carr received his orders rode into camp during the night. Carr also sent Gus Craven, a guide, out into the darkness to find the two troops, under Major Emil Adam, that were patrolling the White River Valley. If it happened that Big Foot had slipped around him, Carr wanted Adam to move up the river to cut off any attempt by the Indians to enter the Stronghold from the northeast.

Big Foot had indeed slipped past Carr. The chief and his band had covered many miles on the night of December 23 at the beginning of their journey for Pine Ridge. The next day, as the column of Indians entered the Badlands, the sun was shining over the eerie landscape, but a bitterly cold wind whipped alkali dust into the faces of people and horses alike. Big Foot lay inside his wagon, ill, his body bouncing roughly in the springless vehicle. Late that afternoon, they reached the Badlands Wall, a sheer cliff, three hundred feet high, that extended for nearly ninety miles along the north bank of the White River. It was broken by only a few passes. Big Foot's band headed for a pass that was seldom used. It was so rough that the warriors had to employ spades and axes to make it passable. The place is still known today as Big Foot Pass and lies six miles west of the present headquarters of Badlands National Monument.

Slowly, painfully, the wagons worked their way down the south side of the Badlands Wall and made an early camp on the south bank of the White River. There, on Christmas Eve, Big Foot's illness developed into pneumonia. Leaving three pickets to watch along the river for soldiers, the caravan broke the White River camp on Christmas Day, moving very slowly because of Big Foot's condition. Upon reaching Cedar Spring, the chief sent three couriers ahead to inform the Pine Ridge chiefs that he was coming. They were to emphasize that he was coming openly and peacefully and that he was very sick. The next day the Indians were able to travel only four miles, camping on Red Water Creek, just inside the boundary of the Pine Ridge Reservation.

By this time army units from Pine Ridge had joined the search for Big Foot. On Christmas Day Major Guy V. Henry and four troops of his buffalo soldiers were sent to cover all approaches to the Stronghold from the east. Everyone still believed Big Foot to be headed for the Stronghold. It was more critical than ever that Big Foot be stopped at this time, for General Brooke's latest peace move was beginning to show some encouraging signs. The five-hundred-man delegation of friendlies the general had decided to send to the Stronghold reported that they found some of the hostiles in a receptive mood. If Big Foot and his band succeeded in reaching the Stronghold, the mood would surely be broken. With their numbers increased by Big Foot's band, and given the news Big Foot would carry about the death of Sitting Bull and the plight of his frightened and scattered people, the hostiles might decide to wage war.

Big Foot's messengers probably reported to the chiefs among the friendlies at Pine Ridge on the morning of December 26, because by noon Brooke knew that the Miniconjous were in the vicinity of Porcupine Creek and headed, not for the Stronghold, but for the agency. It must have been welcome news to the general. He sent out a squadron of the Seventh Cavalry with orders to intercept Big Foot's band, take away the Indians' horses, destroy whatever arms they were carrying, and hold them until he issued further orders.

Brooke then wired Miles in Rapid City and informed him of the action he had taken.

General Miles was extremely pleased and said in his return wire: "Big Foot is cunning and his Indians are very bad. And I hope you will round up the whole body of them, disarm them and keep them under close guard."

Later in the day, Miles's fear that Big Foot might again escape must have grown. He sent Brooke another wire saying,

I have no doubt your orders are all right, but I shall be exceedingly anxious till I know they are executed; whoever secures that body of Indians will be entitled to much credit. They deceived Sumner completely, and if they get a chance they will scatter through the entire Sioux camp or slip out individually.

The Seventh Cavalry, whose job it was to find and capture Big Foot, was commanded by Major Samuel Marmaduke Whitside. He had learned much about Indian fighting during campaigns in the Southwest against the Apaches. With several troops from General Custer's old regiment and an artillery platoon with two Hotchkiss guns, Whitside camped that first evening, December 26, near the trading post at Wounded Knee. Louis Mosseau, the trader, had abandoned his store a month earlier, when it appeared that the dancers, under the leadership of Short Bull and Kicking Bear, might wage war. Mosseau now accompanied Major Whitside back to Wounded Knee Creek and reopened his store. He turned over part of his house, which stood behind the store, to the major and the other officers.

Promptly the next morning, December 27, Whitside sent out a party of Indian scouts, under John Shangreau, the brother of Louis, to search for signs of Big Foot. They went at their task eagerly and with thoroughness, for General Brooke had offered twenty-five dollars to the man who found Big Foot. Another twenty-five dollars had been promised by the bored reporters at Pine Ridge, who had grown weary of trying to invent a war for their editors and readers, and who yearned for a real story. A line of heliographs was set up to connect the Wounded Knee camp with Pine Ridge, and flashing mirrors soon brought further orders from Brooke's aide-de-camp:

I am directed by the Commanding General to say that he thinks Big Foot's party must be in your front somewhere, and that you must make every effort to find him and then move on him at once and with rapidity. There must be a solution reached at the earliest possible moment. Find his trail and follow, or find his hiding place and capture him. If he fights, destroy him.

Those words, flashed by mirrors from ridge to hill and from hill to ridge across the eighteen miles separating Wounded Knee Creek from Pine Ridge Agency, sealed the fate of Big Foot, who at that moment was still camped on Red Water Creek with his band. The chief knew that there were soldiers only forty miles away. During the night one of the couriers he had sent to the chiefs at Pine Ridge had returned and told of the bluecoats he had discovered camped on Wounded Knee Creek at Mosseau's Trading Post. The next morning the other two couriers returned. Bear-Comes-and-Lies and Shaggy Feather reported that the dancers on the Stronghold had been persuaded to surrender. They would reach Pine Ridge in two days, and Kicking Bear and Short Bull wanted Big Foot to time his approach so that all of the Indians would march into the agency on the same day. These two messengers had also discovered the bluecoats on Wounded Knee Creek. They advised their chief to choose a route that would avoid the soldiers. This, however, would mean a longer, harder journey, and Big Foot replied that he was too sick to undertake it. His condition had grown much worse, and he was in great pain. The best thing to do, the chief said, was to go directly and openly to the camp of the soldiers.

The Indian caravan began to move out, and twenty-four hours later, they crossed the divide separating American Horse Creek from Porcupine Creek. A party of warriors riding in advance of the wagons discovered four of Whitside's scouts—Little Bat Garnier; Old Hand, his half-brother; and two Oglalas—watering their horses in the Porcupine. The Miniconjou warriors surrounded the scouts and held them until the rest of the caravan caught up. While the people ate an early lunch, the prisoners were taken to Big Foot. From his sickbed in the wagon, the chief told Old Hand and one of the Oglalas to take word to the commander on Wounded Knee that the Indians were coming peacefully to his camp.

When the two scouts arrived at Whitside's camp, they made their report to the chief of scouts, John Shangreau, who took the news immediately to the major. To Shangreau's dismay, Whitside had "Boots and Saddles" sounded and prepared to leave at once.

Shangreau reminded the major that Big Foot had said he was coming directly to the camp and that the sudden appearance of troops might so confuse and frighten the Miniconjous that trouble would result.

Whitside, in turn, reminded Shangreau that a squadron of the Ninth Cavalry, under Major Guy Henry, was patrolling the area to the north to prevent Big Foot from entering the Stronghold from the east. Ignorant of the latest developments concerning Big Foot and his band, Major Henry and his buffalo soldiers could spoil everything if they suddenly spied the Miniconjous. Whitside wasn't forgetting, either, that Big Foot had slipped away once before after promising to come in. The major did not want to be left waiting, as Colonel Sumner had been five days earlier, and decided that, to be on the safe side, he would march out to meet the chief and escort him back to camp.

By two o'clock that afternoon, Whitside's troops had reached the foot of Porcupine Butte. On the other side of the butte lay the valley of Porcupine Creek, where Old Hand had left the Miniconjous. As Whitside's command paused for a moment, two horsemen came racing down the slope. They were Little Bat and the other Oglala scout who had been released by Big Foot. As the scouts pulled their horses to a stop in front of Major Whitside, the advance guard of the Miniconjou caravan topped the ridge two miles away.

"What kind of mood are they in?" Shangreau asked Little Bat.

"We may be in for some trouble," Little Bat replied.

The troops advanced another mile and then halted. By this time all of the Miniconjous had topped the ridge and moved part way down the slope. The mounted warriors formed a shield in front. Whitside ordered his troops into skirmish formation, gave the command to dismount, and had the two Hotchkiss guns brought out in front of the line. The Miniconjou warriors formed a skirmish line of their own, but there was nothing of military precision in it. Most of the warriors raced back and forth, waving their rifles. Many tied up the tails of their ponies, as was customary before a fight. But behind the warriors, a white flag was in plain sight, flying from a pole on Big Foot's wagon.

All at once the Indians stopped. Two headmen dismounted and started on foot toward the line of bluecoats. Shangreau rode forward to meet them, then went back with them to Big Foot's wagon. A few minutes later, the wagon moved through the line of warriors and drew up before Major Whitside. The officer rode to the side of the wagon and reached down to shake hands with Big Foot. He was shocked by what he saw. The great Miniconjou chief lay in the bed of the wagon, nearly buried under a mound of blankets and robes. Only a small part of his face was exposed. Blood dripped steadily from his nose. Frozen pools of it stained the floorboards; Big Foot had been bleeding for some time.

Through Shangreau, Whitside said, "You must bring your people into my camp on Wounded Knee Creek."

"All right," Big Foot replied weakly. "I am going there. I am going from there to Pine Ridge. The chiefs there have promised to pay me 100 ponies if I come and make peace."

Whitside then told Shangreau to explain to the chief that the Miniconjous must surrender their horses and guns.

The scout protested vigorously. "If you try to take these men's horses and guns, there's liable to be a fight. The men will get away, and some of these women and children will be killed."

"Those were General Brooke's orders," answered Whitside.

"Maybe so," Shangreau said. "But if I were you, I'd get them into the camp first and then take their horses and guns."

Whitside considered the suggestion for a moment and then agreed. Shangreau told Big Foot the major wanted him to move down to the camp on Wounded Knee.

"All right," the sick chief replied. "I am going down to camp. That is where I am going."

Whitside and Big Foot shook hands a second time, and then the major motioned an ambulance forward. The ambulance would be more comfortable, he told the chief, than the springless Indian wagon. After Big Foot was transferred gently to the army vehicle, the cavalrymen remounted and gathered the warriors into a group behind the wagons. At last the cavalcade started off. Two troops of cavalry led the way. Next came the ambulance, followed by the Indian wagons and the mounted warriors. The other two cavalry troops and the two Hotchkiss guns brought up the rear.

Whitside sent a courier racing ahead. A message was to go by heliograph to General Brooke informing him that Big Foot and his entire band of 120 men and 230 women and children had been taken into custody. The major also made the suggestion that Colonel James W. Forsyth and the rest of the regiment, including two more Hotchkiss guns, under the command of Captain Allyn Capron, be sent out to Wounded Knee to help in the disarming. He hoped that if the army put on an overwhelming show of force, Big Foot's warriors would give up their guns peacefully.

The message reached Brooke late that afternoon, and before sunset, Colonel Forsyth was on his way. Brooke had telegraphed the good news to General Miles. He also suggested that, once the prisoners were disarmed, they should be marched to the railroad at Gordon, Nebraska, about twenty-five miles to the southeast, and from there taken to Omaha.

Miles concurred. "All right," his wire said. "Use force enough. Congratulations."

Brooke's instructions to Forsyth, as he later recalled them, were brief: disarm the Indians, take every precaution to prevent their escape, and if they choose to fight, destroy them. As it turned out, this last two-word command was carried out with appalling efficiency. Once the Indians were disarmed, Forsyth was to return to the agency with the First Squadron. Whitside and the Second Squadron were to hold the Miniconjous at Wounded Knee until orders were dispatched to march the Indians to the railroad.

Major Whitside's troops and the Miniconjous reached the camp on Wounded Knee Creek at dusk. The creek meandered northward through a valley that was between three hundred and five hundred yards wide. Just to the east of the creek was a high ridge. On the western edge of the valley were two more ridges, pointing toward the east. Between the two western ridges, a dry ravine wound eastward across the valley to meet the creek. Whitside and the Indians descended the slope on the east, following what was known as the Agency Road. A bridge spanned the creek, and the road continued on, passing the Wounded Knee Post Office and Mosseau's store and continuing south toward the Pine Ridge Agency, eighteen miles away. The cavalry tents stood in rows along the west edge of the road, about one hundred fifty yards south of the bridge. They extended to the base of a low hill that is now called Cemetery Hill.

As the column crossed the bridge, some of the Indians dropped out to enter Mosseau's store and buy coffee, sugar, and other supplies. The rest followed the soldiers past the cavalry tents and made their own camp, as directed, on the north edge of the ravine, below Cemetery Hill. Whitside posted the two Hotchkiss guns on top of the hill and aimed them directly into the Indian camp. He also posted sentinels around the Indian camp.

The major had a large tepee set up for Big Foot at the south side of the cavalry camp. A camp stove was placed inside to heat the tepee and Assistant Surgeon James D. Glennan, with Little Bat as interpreter, was assigned to treat the chief.

Colonel Forsyth arrived with his men about half-past eight and took command. He had led his men east of the

Agency Road, hoping to arrive at the military camp without alarming the Indians, but Lieutenant Charles W. Taylor's troop of Oglala scouts—numbering close to 30—had bivouacked on the south side of the ravine, just across from the Miniconjou camp. They had seen Forsyth arrive and had called the news across the ravine to their kinsmen. The arrival of even more bluecoats spread fear and suspicion through Big Foot's camp. Throughout a restless and largely sleepless night, the Miniconjous grew more uneasy, asking each other why more soldiers had been sent. What was in store for them on the next day?

8

Massacre at Wounded Knee

"Reveille" sounded before sunup. Early rising was routine for the soldiers, but the Indians were late sleepers as a rule. Their early awakening was sweetened, however, by the rations that were distributed among them on the orders of Colonel Forsyth.

When the two squadrons of cavalry turned out at half-past seven, Colonel Forsyth explained his plan to Major Whitside, in command of the First Squadron, and Captain Ilsley, commanding the Second Squadron. He expected no trouble. The Indians were intelligent. They numbered 120 men and 230 women and children. The soldiers numbered a little more than five hundred. Armed resistance on the Indians' part would be foolish and disastrous. Nevertheless, Forsyth wanted to take no chances. He deployed his troops in a hollow square around the Indian village. On Cemetery Hill, in the middle of the north line of troops, he placed the two additional Hotchkiss guns, bringing to a total of four the number of heavy guns pointing down into the Indian camp. B and K troops were stationed inside the square, forming a right angle between the Indian village and the cavalry camp.

The officers were, for the most part, men who had spent years fighting and subduing the Indians. The noncommissioned officers, too, were experienced in Indian warfare. This was not true of the enlisted men, however. Most of them had yet to experience their first action of any kind. Nearly one-fifth of the regiment consisted of raw recruits. Many had come from city slums and were new to the prairie. Thirty-eight had arrived at Pine Ridge only two weeks earlier. The fact that so many of the soldiers had never been under fire and had brought with them from the East a deep fear and distrust of the Indians was a major factor in the tragedy that was about to occur.

As soon as the troops had moved to their assigned positions, Forsyth sent John Shangreau to tell the men of the Indian camp to assemble at Big Foot's tent. Shangreau gave the message to the camp crier, Wounded Hand, who began to walk through the village announcing that the soldier chief wished a council with the men.

The Indians had lost none of the uneasiness they had felt the night before, and Wounded Hand's announcement was followed by rumors to the effect that the soldiers were going to take the Indians' guns away from them. At no time had the men of Big Foot's band contemplated armed resistance to Major Whitside's troops. They had wanted to cooperate as fully as possible so that they could continue their journey to Pine Ridge. But to be asked to surrender their guns was a serious matter. A rifle was a warrior's badge of masculinity and one of his most treasured possessions. He could not easily be persuaded to give it up.

The Indians' reluctance to disarm, however, was more than a matter of pride. The warriors were afraid. There were too many bluecoats surrounding them. Distrustful and suspicious of an enemy who had dealt them so many devastating blows in the past, the Indians feared that, once they gave up their guns, they would be slaughtered by the soldiers. Why else were those "wagon guns" on the hill aimed at their camp?

The Indians' cooperative spirit disappeared at this point. Some of them went to the tent where their sick chief lay tended by Doctor J. Van R. Hoff, medical director for the Seventh Cavalry, who had come with Colonel Forsyth. The restless crowd was constantly on the move—from the tent to the village and back to the tent again. Shangreau, at Colonel Forsyth's request, tried to get the Indian men together and to hold them in one place long enough for the colonel to talk to them.

Finally, Forsyth, Whitside, and Shangreau formed the sullen men into a line facing the entrance to Big Foot's tent. Through Shangreau, the colonel spoke to the Indians in a friendly manner, explaining that their arms must be surrendered. Father M. J. Craft, missionary at Pine Ridge, had accompanied the Seventh Cavalry to Wounded Knee Creek. He later recalled that Colonel Forsyth told the Indians that "they were perfectly safe in the hands of their old friends, the soldiers, and that starvation and other troubles were now happily at an end."

The Indians would have liked nothing better than to have believed that they would never again be hungry and that all their "other troubles were now happily at an end." But how could they take seriously the word of a man who spoke of the soldiers as "their old friends"? Neither the Crows nor the Pawnees nor any other of their ancient enemies had instilled the same terror in their hearts as these soldiers inspired.

The Indians discussed the matter among themselves and then decided to send two men to ask Big Foot's advice. When the chief was told what the colonel had requested, he said, "Give up the bad guns and keep the good ones."

Shangreau, who had come into the tent, too, advised the chief and his men to do as the colonel had asked. "You can always buy guns," said Shangreau, "but if you lose a man, you cannot replace him."

Big Foot, feverish and suffering great pain in his chest, weighed the interpreter's words a few moments and then repeated his original reply: "Keep the good guns."

His two followers went outside and told the other men what their chief had said. When Forsyth heard Shangreau's report of what had taken place inside the tent, he lost no time. He counted off twenty men from the left end of the line of Indians and had Shangreau tell them to go to their lodges and bring back their guns. The men obeyed, but those who remained muttered angrily. The group began to dissolve and reform and dissolve again as individuals wandered off, usually in the direction of the village.

When the twenty men returned, they laid down two rifles —old, broken, and useless. These were the only guns they had, they said. Major Whitside suggested to the colonel that they bring Big Foot outside and command him to order his followers to cooperate. Forsyth agreed. Big Foot was carried out of his tent and laid on the ground. The chief was very weak and still bleeding from the nose. His headmen came forward and sat in a semicircle on the ground behind him.

While this was being done, Forsyth decided to prevent the Indians from leaving the council square and going back into the village. The women and children were becoming excited by the constant passage back and forth. Forsyth placed sentinels between the group of Indian men and the village. All traffic was consequently halted.

Philip Wells replaced Shangreau as interpreter. Forsyth spoke to Big Foot and directed him to tell his men to hand over their guns. The chief replied that they had no guns, that all their arms had been seized and burned by the soldiers at the Cheyenne River Agency.

Forsyth knew this was not true. Whitside had reported that when the band had surrendered the previous day, they had been well armed. There was nothing to do but send soldiers into the village to search the lodges. Captain George D. Wallace and Lieutenant James D. Mann took fifteen men and began the search at the east end of the village. Captain Charles Varnum took fifteen men and began at the other end. Shangreau went with Wallace and Mann as interpreter, Little Bat with Varnum. Major Whitside supervised the search.

The women, cut off from their men, used every trick they could think of to hide the rifles. "The first rifle I found," Varnum was to say later, "was under a squaw who was moaning and who was so indisposed to the search that I had her displaced, and under her was a beautiful Winchester rifle."

In a letter to his brother, written on his deathbed several days later, Lieutenant Mann described his part of the search:

> The enlisted men were not allowed to go inside the tents and took only the arms as we [officers] handed them out. The squaws were sitting on bundles concealing guns and other arms. We lifted them as tenderly and treated them as nicely as possible. Had they been the most refined ladies in the land, they could not have been treated with more consideration. The squaws made no resistance, and when we took the arms they seemed to be satisfied. Wallace played with the children chucking them under the chin and being as pleasant with them as all could be.

The officers took everything that could be considered a weapon—bows and arrows, stone war clubs, hatchets, knives. Some items were found in the wall pockets inside the lodges. Even the wagons the women had packed for the trip to Pine Ridge were unpacked and searched. The result was a fair-sized mound of weapons. Some were carried up Cemetery Hill and deposited near the Hotchkiss guns. Others were tossed into a large tent, near Big Foot's, that was occupied by the scouts.

Separated from their women while the soldiers rummaged through their lodges, not knowing what might come next, the Miniconjou men grew more agitated. A few tried to slip past the sentinels into the village but were turned back.

Ever since the men had first gathered in front of Big Foot's tent that morning, Yellow Bird, the medicine man, had been performing a sort of ceremony. Clad in a Ghost Shirt, blowing on an eagle-bone whistle, he had danced around, muttering his magic words and throwing occasional handfuls of dust into the air in the direction of the soldiers. He began to speak to the Miniconjou men as they squatted or stood in their confined semicircle, facing their chief and his headmen.

"Do not be afraid," he told them, "and let your hearts be strong to meet what is before you. There are many soldiers here, and they have many bullets, but the spirits have told me that the bullets cannot harm us."

The men nodded their heads in approval. Many of them, too, wore the sacred Ghost Shirts that were said to be impervious to the white man's bullets.

When Yellow Bird began to dance again, Interpreter Wells told Major Whitside what the medicine man had said. "He is making mischief," the interpreter warned.

Whitside sent Wells after Colonel Forsyth, and the three men walked over to Yellow Bird and ordered him to sit down. Big Foot's brother-in-law, squatting nearby, heard the command and explained quickly, "He will sit down when he gets around the circle."

Forsyth watched, and when Yellow Bird reached the last man in the semicircle, the medicine man squatted down and lapsed into silence.

By nine-thirty, Captains Wallace and Varnum and Lieutenant Mann had completed their search of the village. Among the knives, axes, and other weapons were thirty-eight rifles. A few were Winchester repeaters; the rest were old, battered, and of little value. Somewhere there was a quantity of Winchesters in excellent condition. Major Whitside and his men had seen the rifles the day before, when Big Foot's band had surrendered. There was only one place the guns could be—under the blankets of the Indian men.

Forsyth, through Interpreter Wells, asked the warriors to come forward voluntarily and hand over the rifles that were hidden under their blankets. Twenty older men came forward immediately and presented themselves to Forsyth, who stood a little to the west of Big Foot's tent and who was flanked by Wallace, Varnum, Whitside, and a detail of six cavalrymen. The younger warriors remained where they were. Yellow Bird got to his feet and began to address them again. One by one the older Miniconjous opened their blankets as they passed Forsyth. Not one of them was concealing a rifle.

Whitside and Varnum then faced each other. The detail of cavalrymen brought some of the young men to their feet and began to herd them past Whitside and Varnum. Of the first three men through the line, two were concealing rifles and cartridge belts. The cartridges were removed, and the belts were returned, empty, to the Indians.

The restiveness of the Indians increased as they witnessed the disarming of their two fellow tribesmen. The Indians' excitement was fed by Yellow Bird's harangue. Interpreter Wells asked Big Foot's brother-in-law to calm the men, but he refused.

The situation was tense. Everyone felt it. Lieutenant Mann later wrote, "I had a peculiar feeling come over me, some presentiment of trouble." He warned his men of K Troop, who were positioned about thirty paces behind the Indian line and parallel to it, to be ready. "There is going to be trouble," he told them. Mann ordered them to fall back about twenty-five feet.

An Indian named Black Coyote began to strut about, holding his rifle over his head with both hands. An Indian policeman who knew him explained later that Black Coyote was a "crazy man, a young man of very bad influence and in fact a nobody." The policeman also said that the man was deaf.

Displaying his rifle defiantly, Black Coyote cried out, "This gun belongs to me! I paid much money for it. I will not give it up unless I am paid for it."

Two soldiers grabbed him from behind, and Black Coyote began to struggle. The gun, pointing eastward and upward at a forty-five-degree angle, went off.

Yellow Bird chose the same instant to throw another handful of dirt into the air. Half a dozen warriors jumped to their feet, threw their blankets aside, and turned their rifles on K Troop behind them.

Whitside, hearing the disturbance as he and Varnum were searching another Indian, glanced up and exclaimed, "My God, they have broken."

It seemed to Lieutenant Mann, facing the rifles of the six warriors, that the Indians hesitated for several heartbeats— long enough for him to think, "The pity of it! What can they be thinking of?" The lieutenant drew his revolver and rushed to the front rank of his troops. The volley from the Indians' rifles spewed into K Troop. "Fire! Fire on them!" Mann yelled.

The lieutenant's command was unnecessary. Instinctively, his men, as well as those of nearby B Troop, opened fire. Nearly half of the assembled warriors went down under the first volley. The other Indians sprang to their feet, throwing their blankets aside as they rose. Although many of them had no rifles, nearly all had revolvers or knives in their belts, and they rushed the line of soldiers. The Indians were so located that every one of their bullets that missed a soldier went singing into their own village. Women and children, frightened out of their wits, ran about seeking cover.

One bullet knocked Captain Varnum's pipe from his mouth. Several went through Doctor Hoff's clothing without harming him. Not all the officers were so fortunate. When firing commenced, Captain Wallace ran to his position behind K Troop. Just as he reached his station, a bullet took off the top of his head.

The fire from B and K Troops was murderous. Big Foot had risen weakly to a sitting position when the fight began. He fell back, shot in the head. The same volley cut down most of the headmen who sat behind the chief.

When the warriors ran out of shells, they broke up into small parties and tried to break through the lines of B and K Troops to get back to their village. This resulted in many hand-to-hand fights. One Indian attacked Interpreter Philip

Wells with a long cheese knife. Wells ducked and threw up his rifle to ward off the blow. The Indian's hand was deflected, but not entirely. The knife sliced across Wells's nose and left it hanging over his mouth by two shreds of skin. The Indian lunged again. This time Wells smashed him behind the ear with his gun. The blow stunned the warrior, and Wells quickly shot him in the side. A corporal who had been watching rushed over and finished off the Indian with a shot to the chest.

With blood streaming down his face, Wells ran for the shelter of a trader's wagon. He slipped, and as he fell, another Indian with a knife jumped on his back. This time only his coat was cut, and Wells tried to fight off his attacker. His dangling nose was such a nuisance that he tried to pull it off, but it would not come loose. Breaking free of the Indian, Wells again made for the trader's wagon, but before he could reach it, bullets grazed the mules and they stampeded, carrying the wagon around the cavalry tents to the base of Cemetery Hill.

Father Craft was moving about giving first aid and administering last rites to the dying. An Indian who came dashing past stopped long enough to plunge a knife into the priest's back. The wound was a serious one. The knife had punctured a lung, but the priest continued to move among the soldiers, helping in any way he could.

The savage hand-to-hand battle lasted no more than five minutes. Most of the Indians broke through the lines of the bluecoats. Some headed east toward G Troop. Most, however, made for the village. As they ran, they turned and fired at the soldiers, who fired back at them. Some of these bullets tore through the tepees, hitting women and children.

The troops forming the square around the battleground had had to stand by helplessly while the fight raged. They dared not fire for fear of hitting the soldiers of B and K Troops. The artillery men on Cemetery Hill stood by their guns, lanyards in hand, unable to fire. Captain Allyn Capron's eye was caught by one of the gunners. The young man was so excited that the captain was afraid he would jerk the lanyard without waiting for the order to fire. Taking no chances, Capron ordered the friction primer removed from the gun.

While the fighting around Big Foot's tent had been going on, most of the Indian women and children had scrambled into the ravine on the south side of their camp. Directly across the ravine, A and I Troops were stationed, dismounted. Their captain ordered them to hold their fire. But close upon the heels of the women and children came the warriors, also heading for the cover of the ravine.

"Here come the bucks!" Captain Henry J. Nowlan yelled. "Give it to them!"

The soldiers opened fire, and the warriors returned it. Behind A and I Troops were a line of Oglala scouts and C and D Troops. These lines now found themselves being fired upon, not only by the Miniconjou warriors, but by the soldiers of B and K Troops who were firing into the rear of the fleeing Indians. In addition to this gunfire, the batteries on Cemetery Hill had opened up, and the shells from at least one of the guns were exploding too close for comfort. The lines of soldiers and Oglala scouts fell back and took new positions.

Suddenly some of the Miniconjou warriors sprang up over the south side of the ravine and headed for the Agency Road. With them were some women and children. Nevertheless, the command was given to fire. An officer later wrote:

> It seemed to me only a few seconds till there was not a living thing before us: warriors, squaws, children, ponies, dogs—for they were all mixed together. . . . I think over thirty bodies were found on our front.

The Indians who remained in the ravine ran in both directions. Some of the warriors who went up the ravine paused to fire at the rear of D Troop, stationed on the ridge to the south. A squad of twelve cavalrymen, under Lieutenant

S. R. H. Tompkins, was sent to stop this fire. The cavalry rode down into the ravine shooting. Three warriors were hit. The others fled. Lieutenant Tompkins later described the brief skirmish.

> A party of squaws and children ran up the ravine not over one hundred yards from my men. I immediately gave the order don't fire on women and children. . . . Behind them, twenty-five or thirty yards from them, came two bucks, stripped and painted, and my men killed these.

The lieutenant and his men continued to fire into the ravine. Meanwhile, the battery on Cemetery Hill was busy. Captain Capron had given his gunners the order to fire when the first warriors had bolted out of the council square, even though they were joined by some women and children from the east end of the Indian village. The Indians had apparently been heading for the agency store. When the artillery shells began to burst among them, they scattered and ran into the field southeast of the store. Here they came under the carbines of G Troop. Those few who escaped this volley of shells and bullets hid beneath the banks of Wounded Knee Creek, to the north.

At the other end of the Indian village, women and children jumped into their wagons, which were already harnessed for what they had thought was to be the final leg of their journey to Pine Ridge. The wagons went hurtling up the Agency Road to the northwest, almost lost in the dust of the stampeding pony herd that preceded them. The route of the wagons passed under the guns of E Troop, which occupied the low hill to the right of Cemetery Hill. Lieutenants Horatio Sickel and Sedgwick Rice hurriedly ordered their men to dismount and deployed them to cover the road. As the seething mass approached, both officers noticed that it was made up entirely of women and children and shouted orders to their men not to fire. "Shoot the stampeding ponies!" they commanded instead. As the troops carried out this command, an old woman on horseback fired at the line of bluecoats.

"There is a buck!" shouted one of the troopers as the woman drew into his sights.

"No, it's a squaw," Lieutenant Rice shouted back. "Don't shoot her."

"Well, by God, Lieutenant, she is shooting at us," retorted the soldier, but he turned his carbine back into the pony herd.

The women and children in the jolting wagons were allowed to escape unhurt up the road.

Not all the Indians had left the village, however. Scattered shots came from the tepees. Some of the big guns on Cemetery Hill were turned on the camp. Their fire shredded the canvas lodges. Nearly everyone left in the village was killed. One woman, Blue Whirlwind, received fourteen shrapnel wounds from the bursting shells. Her two little boys, huddled by her side, were also wounded. All three survived. Another woman, badly wounded, crawled out of her tepee toward a wounded soldier with a knife in her teeth. The white man saw her and screamed just as she plunged the knife into him. Another soldier heard the scream and shot the woman. She fell dead on top of her victim.

The man most directly responsible for the holocaust, Yellow Bird, sought cover in the large, conical tent belonging to the scouts that stood on the edge of the council square at the south side of the cavalry camp. Yellow Bird had a gun—either his own or one he had picked up. Slitting a hole in the canvas, he began to fire at the soldiers of B and K Troops. He shot several before the source of the fire was discovered. A private of K Troop started to run toward the tent.

"Come back!" shouted Lieutenant Mann.

Ignoring the command, the private slashed open the tent with a knife. Yellow Bird turned his gun on the soldier. The blast caught the private in the stomach.

"My God, he has shot me," the boy exclaimed. "I am killed. I am killed." He lunged back out of the tent and started toward his lieutenant; but he fell forward, dead.

The private's comrades fired volley after volley from their carbines into the tent. A Hotchkiss gun spat two shells directly into it. Other soldiers then rushed forward, piled bales of hay around the tent, and set them afire. In moments the tent had burned to the ground. Yellow Bird's body lay exposed, shattered by bullets and shrapnel, charred by fire.

Most of the fighting, however, centered on the ravine, about one hundred fifty feet wide and running almost straight east and west for nearly half a mile through the main battle area. The gully was a nightmare of confusion and terror, death and pain. In that dreadful maelstrom, the experience of Dewey Beard, a Miniconjou warrior, was typical. In the first moments of the fight in the council square, the Indian had rushed a bluecoat in an attempt to capture a gun. Sinking his knife into the soldier, he made off with his carbine and dodged through K Troop and the Indian village and into the ravine. The warrior was fired upon by the troops on the south side of the ravine, and a bullet caught him in the arm, knocking him down. A nearby soldier fired, but his gun was empty. Dewey Beard quickly aimed at the soldier and pulled the trigger, but the Indian's carbine, too, was empty. As he sprang to his feet and started down the slope into the ravine, another bullet hit him "in the lap," as he recalled later. Dewey Beard sank down and reloaded. From the bottom of the ravine, he began to fire at the bluecoats, although he could see only dimly through the dust and smoke on the south edge of the gully. Suddenly, a shell stuck in the chamber of his gun. Soldiers on both sides of the ravine were firing at him. He got up and began to run west up the gully.

An old Indian, crouching under the lip of the ravine, gave Dewey Beard a Springfield rifle. Two other warriors joined him, and they charged up the south bank into the fire of the soldiers. The other two warriors dropped. Dewey Beard dived back into the ravine and found himself face to face with an Oglala scout. Both fired; both missed, but Dewey Beard fell

back, weakened by his wounds. The scout, believing Dewey
Beard dead, ran on.

Dewey Beard lay there for a few moments, trying to re-
cover his strength. He saw women and children trying to
climb out of the ravine and being cut down by fire from the
soldiers. Some mothers dug holes in the bank with their bare
hands and thrust their babies in them to keep them safe
from the bullets that laced the air.

Continuing on west up the ravine, Dewey Beard came
upon his mother, badly wounded. She thrust the soldier's
pistol she was holding into Dewey Beard's hand. "Go on,
my son," she said. "I am going to fall down now." Another
bullet hit her, and she dropped at his feet, dead.

By this time Dewey Beard had used up all the cartridges
he had for the Springfield. From another old man, he obtained a fully loaded Winchester and continued up the
ravine, looking now for his wife. He found William, his
brother, and White Lance, his best friend. William was
propped against the bank, a hole in his chest. White Lance
was wounded, too. Somehow the three men made their way
farther up the ravine to a point where it turned sharply and
formed a pocket. Several other warriors were already there,
firing at E Troop and the battery on Cemetery Hill. Dewey
Beard, his brother, and his friend joined the warriors at the
top of the slope.

The Indians' fire drew a vicious barrage of bullets and
shells. Dust rose like smoke around them. They were scarcely
able to see or breathe. A Hotchkiss shell punched a six-inch
hole in the stomach of a warrior near Dewey Beard. A bullet
thudded into the dirt a few inches from Dewey Beard's face
and threw dirt into his eyes. He slid back down the bank.
Up and down the ravine, he heard the women singing death
songs.

On Cemetery Hill, the gunners concentrated on wiping
out this last pocket of resistance. Corporal Paul H. Weinert
and several men moved a Hotchkiss gun from Cemetery Hill
to the lower hill on the west, which was being held by E

Troop. This put the gun about three hundred yards from the pocket. The Indians opened fire on the gunnery crew immediately. One of the soldiers went back to Cemetery Hill for ammunition and never returned.

Weinert's captain called him back; but the corporal ignored the order and kept moving the gun closer to the Indians, shooting as he went. Second Lieutenant Harry L. Hawthorne started toward Weinert, also ordering him back. Suddenly, Hawthorne went down. "Oh, my God!" he exclaimed.

One of the gunners ran to him and carried him to cover behind the hill.

"I'll make them pay for that!" Weinert cried and ran the gun almost up to the bank of the ravine.

The Hotchkiss gun grew hot, and Weinert kept yelling for someone to bring one of the other guns down from Cemetery Hill. He and his crew were so close to the Indians in the pocket that their clothing and the wheels of the gun were bored full of holes. Once a bullet knocked a cartridge out of Weinert's hand just as he was about to insert it in the gun. Miraculously, it did not explode.

Colonel Forsyth ordered Lieutenant Rice to take his platoon of E Troop to the southwest and begin to clear out the ravine. With troops pressing them from the west and the Hotchkiss belching down into their midst, the Indians scattered from the pocket.

Dewey Beard started up the ravine, still looking for his wife, but was forced to climb out and flee to the south and west when he ran into Rice's platoon. Dewey Beard's wife, Wears Eagle, was later found dead, shot in the chest. Their twenty-five-day-old daughter, Wet Feet, was still nursing at her mother's breast. The baby died three months later. Her father claimed her death was due to the fact that she had swallowed so much blood. Dewey Beard lost both parents and two brothers, William and Sherman, besides his wife and baby.

Interpreter Philip Wells, whose severed nose still dangled over his mouth, went to the edge of the ravine and called out,

"All of you that are still alive get up and come on over; you will not be molested or shot."

After a few moments, the wounded people crawled from the ravine and allowed the soldiers to guide them to the hospital area north of the cavalry camp.

From the ravine Wells moved into the council square, where the fight had begun. It was now littered with Miniconjou bodies. "These white people came to save you," he called out in the Sioux language, "and you have brought death upon yourselves. Still, the white people are merciful . . . so if some of you are alive, raise your heads. I am a man of your own blood who is talking to you."

About a dozen of the fallen Miniconjous raised their heads. One of them motioned Wells to his side. Pointing to the burned and shattered body that lay within the ruins of the scouts' tent, he asked whose body it was.

"It is Yellow Bird," Wells told him.

"He raised himself a little higher," Wells related afterward,

raised his closed fist, pointing it toward the dead Indian, shot out his fingers, which is amongst Indians a deadly insult, meaning I could kill you and still not be satisfied doing it, am sorry I could do no more to you, and then used words tremblingly which I could not all catch, but he said this which I did hear, speaking as though to the dead man: "If I could be taken to you I would stab you," then turning to me said, "he is our murderer; only for him exciting our young men we would have all been alive and happy."

One detail of cavalrymen was sent to round up the Indian pony herd, which was grazing about a mile west of Cemetery Hill. Captain Edward S. Godfrey was ordered to take some of his men from D Troop and follow the ravine two miles west to its head in search of any Indians who might have escaped.

With fourteen men, Godfrey reconnoitered the area to the west, riding up the crest of a divide and then descending into a small creek valley. Here an alarm was given. Indians had been seen running into the dense brush along the creek.

Godfrey cautiously led forward a dismounted skirmish line. "How, Cola," he called, using the Indian words of friendship. "Squaw, papoose. Cola. How, Cola."

Nothing but silence answered Godfrey's call. He moved his men closer to the brush. "How, Cola. Squaw. Papoose," he said, inviting any Indian women and children to come forward in safety. But there was no response. "Ready," commanded Godfrey. "Fire." The stillness was broken by the crack of rifles and a scream.

"Cease firing!" Godfrey commanded quickly. He ran into the brush. An Indian woman and two children lay dying. A fourth figure, which Godfrey took to be man, lay on his face as if dead.

As the squad turned to leave, Blacksmith Carey noted some movement and said, "Hey, this man ain't dead." As Carey made the statement, he put the muzzle of his rifle to the Indian's head and pulled the trigger. Turning the body over, the squad saw that it was a boy of fourteen or fifteen.

Captain Godfrey was upset and asked Carey why he had shot the boy. Carey, upset, too, and frightened, began to cry. He replied that he had thought only of self-defense.

"I had been warned not to trust a wounded Indian, or take any chances with one. I shot without thinking," Carey later recalled. He had been a soldier for only a few weeks at the time of the battle.

Captain Henry Jackson and the thirty-four men of C Troop who had been sent after the pony herd spied an Indian sliding into the ravine about a mile beyond the herd and went after him. In fact, there were twenty-five Miniconjous hiding there in the shelter of an overhang. Eight were men. The rest were women and children. When the soldiers rode up, they could see only rifles pointing out of the brush toward them. At first there was no way of determining that women and children were hiding in the overhang. Troops and Indians began firing. Captain Jackson sent a lieutenant with a detail down the ravine to prevent the Indians' escape and then began to close in.

Reinforcements arrived unexpectedly. Captain Winfield S. Edgerly had been sent by Colonel Forsyth to round up all Indians who had escaped to the west. Edgerly joined Jackson, who posted the newcomers on the opposite side of the Indians. A few Oglala scouts had accompanied Edgerly, and one of them informed Jackson that there were women and children in the group and that some were his own relatives. The scout was certain he could coax the fugitives out. Jackson ordered a cease fire and pulled his men back a short distance. The scouts moved cautiously toward the overhang and shouted down to the fugitives that if they surrendered, they would not be harmed.

But the Miniconjous were so frightened that Jackson had to withdraw all his men and the Oglalas had to coax for half an hour before their kinsmen would come out. A pathetic group of Indians finally crawled out of their makeshift fort. Soldiers helped the injured—four men, three women, and a child—carrying them out of the ravine and administering first aid. Fifteen or sixteen rifles were found in the refuge. An ambulance was sent for, and Edgerly left with his men and the scouts to pick up the pony herd. Jackson and his detail remained with the prisoners. While Jackson waited for an ambulance, Captain Godfrey and the fourteen men of D Troop rode up, returning from their search of the creek valley to the west. As Jackson and Godfrey talked, six mounted Indians rode in from the west. Noting that one of them wore the badge of an agency policeman, Jackson relaxed. The Indians approached and shook hands with Jackson and Godfrey, and Jackson observed a party of mounted Indians forming on a hill to the northwest. After shaking hands with the white men, the six Indians turned and rode back as if to join the other Indians. About seventy-five yards away, they wheeled. Five of them began firing at the troops. The policeman shouted and apparently tried to stop them, but without success. One of Godfrey's men slumped to the ground, wounded.

The Indians on the hill, numbering about one hundred fifty, charged the troops from three directions. Jackson ordered the prisoners abandoned and the troops to retreat down the opposite side of the divide. At the bottom of the slope, they rallied and loosed a volley as the Indians charged over the hill. One warrior was killed, two wounded. The others wheeled, rode back to the top of the ridge, gathered up the Miniconjou prisoners, and rode off to the west.

The rescuers of the Miniconjous were Oglalas and Brules from the Pine Ridge Agency who, when they heard the sounds of the guns from Wounded Knee Creek, had rushed to the aid of their Miniconjou kinsmen.

Black Elk had gone out after his horses that morning when he heard the shooting. He had slept very little the night before the battle. Black Elk had seen Colonel Forsyth leave with most of the rest of the Seventh Cavalry to join Major Whitside on Wounded Knee. Watching the additional troops move out, Black Elk felt that "something terrible was going to happen."

When he heard the guns firing to the east the next morning, Black Elk turned back to his camp. A man rode up to him and said, "Hey-hey-hey! The people that are coming [Big Foot and his band] are fired on! I know it."

Black Elk quickly saddled his pony and donned his sacred shirt. Painted on the back was a spotted eagle with outspread wings; the left shoulder was decorated with the daybreak star. Across the breast, from left shoulder to right hip, was a flaming rainbow. Around the neck was painted another rainbow, like a necklace, with a star at the bottom. An eagle feather was tied at each shoulder, elbow, and wrist, and over the entire shirt, red streaks of lightning blazed.

Still hurrying, spurred on by the distant sounds of artillery fire, Black Elk painted his face red and tied a single eagle feather in his hair.

He started out alone, unarmed except for a sacred bow he had made as a result of the vision he had had as a boy. He was soon overtaken by 150 warriors from Two Strike's band who, only two weeks before, had been persuaded to leave the Stronghold and come into the agency. They had all painted themselves for war and rushed toward the sound of the guns.

As the party drew near the battleground, an Indian rider came galloping toward them from that direction and cried, "Hey-hey-hey! They have murdered them!" Then he whipped his horse and dashed away to Pine Ridge to carry the dark news.

As they came to the top of one of the ridges on the west side of the battleground, Black Elk and the warriors had a clear view of the ravine, that inferno of confusion, blood, pain, and death. Black Elk never forgot his horror at the sight of the torn and crumpled bodies of women and children. Directly ahead of them, Captain Jackson was collecting the small group of Miniconjous he had flushed out of the shelter of the overhang.

Black Elk said to his companions, "Take courage. These are our relatives. We will try to get them back." Then he led them in a song:

> A thunder-being nation I am, I have said.
> A thunder-being nation I am, I have said.
> You shall live,
> You shall live,
> You shall live,
> You shall live.

Riding over the ridge, they called to one another, "Take courage! It is time to fight!"

Jackson and his men returned empty-handed to the battlefield. Forsyth was alarmed at the report that agency Indians had ridden over to join the fight. A wagon train had just arrived with supplies sent by General Brooke from Pine Ridge, and Forsyth arranged the wagons in a barricade around the artillery position on Cemetery Hill. By noon, however, it became apparent that the agency Indians were not going to attack, and the troops were dispatched to clean up the battlefield. Ambulances were sent around to collect the wounded soldiers and Indians for treatment at the field hospital that had been hurriedly set up near the cavalry camp. Not all the wounded Indians were found. Some had crawled away to hide wherever they could, either to die or to escape after the soldiers had pulled out.

The wounded were loaded onto the supply wagons for the ride back to the agency. To provide as much comfort as was possible in the springless vehicles, the floors were padded with sacks of grain covered with straw. One ambulance carried two badly wounded lieutenants. The other carried Father Craft and a sergeant.

At last, late in the afternoon, the Seventh Cavalry began the return trip to Pine Ridge. Silently witnessing the departure were the corpses of Big Foot and most of his people. The chief, his body frozen in a grotesque half-sitting position, seemed to be waving goodbye.

9

A People's Dream Dies

WHEN MOUNTED couriers came rushing into the Pine Ridge Agency with news of the slaughter at Wounded Knee, the Sioux were terrified. They had been uneasy from the first dark moment, weeks earlier, when troops had appeared on their reservation. Upon learning of the terrible battle, they could think of nothing but escape. The Indians tore down their lodges and fled.

In the chapel, where a twenty-five-foot cedar tree had been set up, some of the white women of the agency were hanging decorations and filling bags of candy in preparation for a belated observance of Christmas. Elaine Goodale, the schoolteacher, stood near a window in the chapel and watched the Indians flee.

"Their white camps melted away like snow-banks in April," she wrote. "The brown hills were instantly alive with galloping horsemen and a long line of loaded wagons disappeared in the distance."

General Brooke and Agent Royer did everything they could to calm and reassure the Indians, but without success. The flight of the Sioux was hastened when Black Elk and the 150 warriors from Two Strike's band returned and told of the massacre that had occurred at Wounded Knee. In contrast to their terrified audience, the inclination of Two Strike's warriors was not to flee the agency in search of safety. They wanted to fight. They swarmed back and forth like a cloud of angry hornets over the ridge southwest of the agency. Finally, one of the warriors, a man named Turning Bear, dashed across the creek on his pony to set fire to the agency barn. The Indian police, who had been watching, charged him. Turning Bear fired at them twice, and they returned a furious volley that drove him back across the creek and up the ridge. Almost immediately, General Brooke appeared on the scene with Doctor Eastman. "Stop, stop!" the general shouted. "Doctor, tell them they must not fire until ordered!"

Eastman interpreted the injunction, and the police stopped firing.

Thomas Henry Tibbles, a correspondent for the *Omaha World Herald*, was at that moment returning to the agency from the battlefield to send a story off to his editor. He found the agency in a panic. Fleeing women and children, white and Indian, were bunching among the buildings.

Suddenly a Sioux warrior, wearing a Ghost Shirt and full war paint, came riding slowly down the main road, shouting something in the Sioux language. Tibbles could not understand what the man was saying, but he saw the quartermaster's Indian assistants leave their work and disappear. Continuing to cry his announcement at the top of his lungs, the warrior rode among the buildings. When he came upon a small band of soldiers drawn up in an open space just south of the main buildings, the Indian circled them, careful that they should all hear him. Because the warrior was unarmed and made no menacing moves, the soldiers, in turn, made no move to molest him. After the man had ridden around the main part of the agency, crying his message, he spurred his horse and rode back to the hills where the rest of the warriors had gathered.

Tibbles sought out an Indian woman who could speak English and asked her what the man had said.

"He said," she replied, " 'Prepare to fight! We are going to shoot into the agency.' "

A few minutes later, the Indians did indeed begin firing into the agency. It was long-range fire, and most of the bullets fell harmlessly, but the panic inside the confines of the agency grew. The civilians were convinced that the Sioux were getting ready to attack, and there were only a few soldiers present to defend them. Most of the Seventh Cavalry had been sent to Wounded Knee to disarm and capture Big Foot. The buffalo soldiers of the Ninth Cavalry had been sent out the day before Christmas to scout the Badlands to the northwest in search of Big Foot, who at that time had not yet been located. The only troops remaining to defend the agency were a few men of the Seventh Cavalry and some of the Second Infantry.

Tibbles hurried to his lodgings to see to the safety of his wife. Not finding her there, he searched for her in the crowd of women and children gathering among the buildings. There he found her.

Susette La Flesche Tibbles, daughter of Iron Eye, former head chief of the Omahas, was standing on a box and calling out to the women, "Why do you come here? These thin-board buildings cannot protect you from bullets. You must go to the log houses."

Bright Eyes, as she was called by nearly everyone who knew her, soon had the women and children safely tucked away in the log houses.

In the chapel where Elaine Goodale was working, a similar scene of terror and panic was being enacted. Soon after the couriers had brought the news of the massacre at Wounded Knee, wrote the teacher, the

chapel and mission house were swamped by a crowd of sobbing, terrified women and children—church members, for the most part of mixed descent. The two Presbyterian missionary women left their more exposed cottage on the brow of the hill and joined us in the rectory, one of them carrying her pet canary in his cage. The solid outside shutters were slammed to, the oil lamps lit, and an effort made to calm the excitement with the help of hot coffee and sandwiches.

Tibbles, after sending his editor a brief account of the day's events by way of a courier to Rushville—correspondents were forbidden the use of the army telegraph at the agency—went to the place where the troops were lined up awaiting the expected attack. From where they stood, the soldiers could see the Sioux swarming all over the ridge on their ponies, sunlight glinting on their rifle barrels.

Tibbles sat down on a nearby cracker box and began to take notes. Occasionally, a puff of dust flew up as a bullet struck the ground not far away. As the reporter sat there, a young soldier came by with a camp stove on his back. Suddenly, the boy's hat flew off. He set the stove down, replaced his hat on his head, and started on. He had taken only a few steps when he became suspicious. He set the stove back down, removed his hat, and examined it. Then he began to run. An officer ordered him to halt, went up to the soldier, and examined the hat himself. It had been pierced by a bullet. The officer exhibited it to the troops as a warning, returned it to the soldier, and told him to get on with his errand.

The bullets that were falling within the agency were coming from a group of warriors who had hidden themselves in a deep gulch to the north. After a while their firing became continuous and posed a serious hazard to those inside the agency. A company of infantry in particular danger from the fire was ordered to take cover behind some stacked cordwood north of the buildings. Three soldiers were hit before the company reached the woodpiles. A young newspaper photographer rushed to the wounded men and began taking pictures while bullets whined around him. When he ignored an officer's order to leave, the photographer was placed under arrest.

General Brooke gave no orders to return the fire from the

gulch. After a while Lieutenant A. W. Corliss went to Brooke
and asked permission to fire into the gulch with his Hotchkiss gun. Brooke refused. He hoped to coax the Sioux back
into their campsites, believing that the majority of them,
though excited, were not hostile and did not want to fight
the soldiers.

Among the defenders of the fort were nearly eighty Indian policemen. Agent Royer and some of his assistants did
not trust them and had previously maintained that if trouble
should start, the policemen would turn their guns against
the whites within the agency. The Indian police had been
deployed in a line west of headquarters, and their officer
had had a difficult time restraining them from returning the
fire from the gulch. When the company of infantry came
under fire as they ran for cover behind the cordwood, the
Indian police could be restrained no longer. Breaking away
from their officer, they charged the warriors in the gulch.
Within moments they had cleared out the hostiles. Then,
finally heeding their officer's command, the police returned
to their line.

Within the agency, occasional firing was heard until sun-
down. Most of the civilians did not share General Brooke's
opinion that the majority of the Sioux out in the hills were
friendly and merely excited and uncertain. The civilians
expected a full-scale attack, and tension ran high. Doctor
Eastman, a Sioux himself, feared an attack. His office was
full of people seeking refuge. He persuaded one of the
refugees to lend Elaine Goodale—who had consented on
Christmas day to marry him—a horse and to accompany her
to the railroad and safety. But Miss Goodale refused to
leave, choosing instead to stay and give what aid she could.

Although they didn't realize it, the civilians' fears of an
attack were groundless. The warriors who swarmed over
the hills during the afternoon—numbering several hundred—could have overrun the agency in half an hour if
they had wanted to. But they never had planned to attack.
They were simply providing a rear guard for their families,

who were either hiding in the hills or fleeing toward the safety of the Badlands. About dusk, the warriors left and headed north to join their families. General Brooke had managed to coax in only a few.

As the Indians left, they stopped at Red Cloud's cabin and forced the old chief to accompany them. His power dissipated by many years of cooperating with the whites, Red Cloud could neither prevent his own abduction nor persuade the Indians to return to the agency.

In the valley of White Clay Creek, about fifteen miles northwest of the agency, the fleeing horde met Short Bull, Kicking Bear, and their followers, who were on their way to the agency to surrender. When the two Ghost Dance apostles were told what had happened to Big Foot's band, they changed their minds. The entire group, numbering close to four thousand people, including eight hundred to one thousand warriors, camped on White Clay Creek. Through the night survivors of Wounded Knee drifted or staggered in, many of them injured. Sounds of mourning were heard throughout the encampment. Some of the dancers began a Ghost Dance.

The leaders of the fugitives went into council. According to Red Cloud, they "made a law, that no one should go back to the agency. All rather die together. I tried my best for them to let me go back, but they would not let me go, and said if I went they would kill me."

At nine-thirty that evening, the Seventh Cavalry arrived back at the agency. With them they brought their own casualties and thirty-three severely wounded Miniconjous, all but six of them women and children. Colonel Forsyth stopped at headquarters to report to General Brooke. The troops headed for camp, fed and watered their horses, and rolled up in their blankets. Although they were exhausted, they slept uneasily. No one knew what the fugitive Sioux were planning.

The wounded were taken to a field hospital that had been set up by Lieutenant Colonel Dallas Bache, the medical

director. But the hospital could accommodate only sixty patients. The injured soldiers and thirteen wounded Sioux—
four of them men—were admitted. There was no room for
the rest of the wounded—mostly women and children. They
were handed over to Major Edmund Butler, who could think
of no place to take them. Thomas Tibbles suggested that the
Reverend Charles Cook, himself a full-blooded Sioux, might
permit his Episcopal church to be used as a makeshift
hospital. Cook agreed at once. When the three men went
to the church together to see what needed to be done to
accommodate the wounded, Tibbles found the chapel still
decorated with Christmas greens. Above the pulpit hung
a large banner that read: "Peace on earth, good will to men."

Major Butler ordered the pews torn out and the floor
covered with hay.

"Quilts were brought from the house," Elaine Goodale
wrote later, and the victims were

> lifted from the wagons and tended throughout the night by
> Doctor Eastman, the physician of their own blood, with such
> volunteer help as was available. Later one of the Army surgeons
> came to assist, but no one wondered to see the Sioux women
> shrink in horror from the dreaded uniform. We made gallons
> of coffee, and distributed bread to as many as were able to eat.

One woman, when told that her Ghost Dress had to be
removed in order for her wound to be dressed, replied: "Yes,
take it off. They told me a bullet would not go through it.
Now I don't want it anymore."

Tibbles declared that nothing he had seen in his entire
life affected or depressed him as did the sights he saw in
the church that night

> under the festival decorations of the Prince of Peace, which hung
> above the rows of suffering, innocent women and children. For
> all their agony not one of them uttered a word of complaint. In
> fact the only sound in the place was the voice of a little three-
> year-old girl who stood near the entrance, beside the one un-

wounded old woman, who held a baby on her lap. Though the grandmother tried to hush her, the little child kept saying slowly over and over, "Min-nie, min-nie, min-nie," which I knew was the Sioux word for water.

There was no water there yet. I went out and fetched a bucketful and a tin cup. As the child looked frightened at seeing a white man coming so near her, I handed a cup of water to the old woman, telling her to give it to the child, who grabbed it as if parched with thirst. As she swallowed it hurriedly, I saw it gush right out again, a bloodstained stream, through a hole in her neck.

Tibbles went to the army hospital to plead with the surgeon, Major Hartsuff, to come at once and administer to the wounded in the church. The major, who had his hands full tending the injured soldiers, promised to come as soon as he could and gave Tibbles some morphine to ease the pain of the most seriously wounded of the Indians. Concerned about four nursing babies whose mothers had been killed and who had been without food since morning, Tibbles asked if there was anything the major could give him for the infants. Hartsuff gave him two bottles of beef extract. He directed Tibbles to make hot soup with the beef extract and to feed the soup to the babies. The concoction might harm a tiny white baby, Hartsuff said, but "the Indians have lived on meat for ages, and their babies will grow fat on it."

It was two o'clock in the morning before Major Hartsuff could leave his own men and come to the church. Tibbles greeted him, and for a moment the officer stood just inside the door, looking at the rows of wounded and dying women and children. The silence was awesome. Not a sigh or a groan was to be heard.

Then, to Tibbles's amazement, the military surgeon, who had served during the Civil War and was no stranger to the sight of battle wounds, grew pale and faint. He sat down abruptly on the straw-covered floor.

"What's the matter?" Tibbles asked anxiously.

Weakly the major replied, "This is the first time I've seen a lot of women and children shot to pieces. I can't stand it."

Hartsuff went outside and sat on a log. Tibbles brought him a cup of coffee, and a few minutes later, the surgeon reentered the church and set to work helping Doctor Eastman. Most of the wounds were severe enough to require surgery, but nothing could persuade the suffering women to allow an army surgeon to operate on them. As a result, most of the patients died.

After Major Hartsuff appeared in the church, the old Indian woman who had been caring for the child with the hole in her throat asked Mrs. Tibbles, who was helping to tend the wounded, "When will they kill us?"

Mrs. Tibbles explained that the doctor was there to help make them well and that white people did not kill prisoners or women and children.

The Indian woman could not believe it. "But we saw them kill and wound all those women and children today," she said. "We know they have brought us in here to make a feast and then to kill us."

Mrs. Tibbles—Bright Eyes—then went about the room assuring the Indians that they would not be killed, that everything possible would be done to ease their suffering, and that they would be fed when they were hungry. Gradually, they accepted her assurances. Up to that moment, they had maintained their stoic silence, for it was not their custom to let their enemies hear them cry out in pain or fear. Persuaded that these whites were not their enemies, the wounded began to moan and cry so pitifully that those who heard them could scarcely bear it.

Preparing for a possible attack upon the agency, General Brooke sent out a pair of Indian scouts with orders to Major Guy V. Henry to return to the agency with his squadron of buffalo soldiers. At nine o'clock that night, the scouts rode into Major Henry's camp, fifty miles north of Pine Ridge, on White River opposite the mouth of Wounded Knee

Creek. The troopers themselves had returned to camp only two hours previous to the arrival of the scouts. The soldiers had just completed a taxing, fifty-mile scout of the Stronghold, which they had found deserted.

The tired soldiers broke camp, loaded their wagons, and set out for the night ride to Pine Ridge. They huddled in their buffalo overcoats and muskrat caps against the biting wind and light snow. Major Henry pushed his exhausted men and horses, hoping to reach what might be a beleaguered agency by daybreak. When he found that the wagons were slowing him up, he left them behind with Captain John S. Loud's I Troop as escort. Pushing onward as fast as the horses could go, Major Henry arrived at the agency shortly before dawn. His men finally bedded down just as "Reveille" was sounded for the Seventh Cavalry.

Only minutes later, one of Captain Loud's men came riding hard into Pine Ridge to report that the wagon train had been attacked by Indians two miles east of the agency. Lieutenant Preston's Oglala scouts started out immediately, followed closely by the Seventh Cavalry. When they arrived on the scene, they found the wagons had been formed into a hollow square. The troopers were being fired upon from a nearby hill by forty or fifty Indians. At the sight of the relief column, the warriors vanished. One corporal had been killed in the brief skirmish. Escorted by the scouts and cavalry, the wagon train proceeded in safety to Pine Ridge.

The war party that had attacked the wagon train had been sent out by the chiefs from the fugitive camp on White Clay Creek solely to observe the strength and activities of General Brooke's forces. The chiefs had warned the young men not to start a fight. But the braves were too worked up over the events of the last twenty-four hours to resist seizing an opportunity for revenge. Withdrawing hastily when they caught sight of the Seventh Cavalry, the warriors started northward toward Father Jutz's Holy Rosary Mission and School, more commonly known as the Drexel Mission. The kindly German priest had won the affection and respect of all the Indians on Pine Ridge. The hostiles had sent word to him that they would harm nothing and no one within the mission. As a result, about twenty persons who lived in the neighborhood had taken refuge there. The Sisters of St. Francis and Mrs. Philip Wells, the wife of the interpreter and herself a schoolteacher, stood at the gate offering meat and coffee to Indians who were fleeing the agency and heading for the fugitive camp.

Although the warriors kept their promise not to harm the mission or anyone in it, their blood was too hot to permit them to pass through the area without venting some of their fury. They set fire to a small log cabin that Mrs. Wells used as a schoolhouse, then rode on down the valley.

Four miles away at the agency, the smoke from the burning cabin was seen. Fearing that the mission was burning, General Brooke ordered out the Seventh Cavalry. He also told Major Henry to be ready in case the Ninth Cavalry was needed. Forsyth's Seventh Cavalry and an artillery platoon started for the mission without taking time to breakfast. They were followed by Lieutenant Preston and ten Oglala scouts, including Philip Wells, whose nose had been sewn back in place, John and Louis Shangreau, Little Bat, and Joe Merrivale. Although they soon saw that only the schoolhouse was burning, they went on to the mission. Here the soldiers eagerly accepted the meat and coffee the sisters had earlier been handing out to the fleeing Indians.

While Colonel Forsyth and Father Jutz talked, the colonel noticed two more columns of smoke rising over the valley to the north. It was Father Jutz's guess that another log schoolhouse and a shed had been set afire.

Because there were no Indians in sight and the mission appeared to be safe from harm, Forsyth decided there was nothing more that could be done there. He sent a message to General Brooke advising that he was returning and that there was no need to send Major Henry and his tired men.

The courier had no sooner left, however, than Little Bat reported to Colonel Forsyth that he heard gunfire down the creek. Forsyth knew the hostile camp lay in that direction. He also knew there was another line of troops on White River. Suspecting that the two forces had clashed, he decided to push down the valley.

The valley of White Clay Creek, in which the Drexel Mission was located, was three hundred yards wide. On the east steep bluffs rose two hundred feet high. The bluffs on the west were only about fifty feet high and gave way to a low plateau. The road the troops followed crossed the creek and then began to ascend this low table of land.

Preston's scouts, ahead of the troops, ran into a small group of warriors on the plateau. The hostiles called out, "You scouts turn back. We don't want to fight you. We want to fight the soldiers."

The scouts retreated immediately and reported to Preston. The lieutenant wanted the scouts to go back and count the warriors, but they refused. So Preston cautiously climbed up to the crest himself and counted about twenty warriors, approximately one hundred yards directly in front of him. He fired two shots at them.

By this time Forsyth had come up behind Preston with one squadron. Forsyth ordered some of the men to dismount and hold the position. The colonel deployed the remainder of the squadron in a skirmish line below. The horse handlers led the horses to a spot where the animals would be out of the paths of flying bullets.

For a couple of hours, the two forces exchanged long-range fire. The only army casualty was a trooper who received a bullet in the foot. But Forsyth had made a serious blunder. He had not sent men to secure the bluffs on either side above him, and gradually the Indians had worked themselves into these positions. Although their fire was still long-range and, at least for the moment, not very dangerous, the Indians could eventually close in and make things very hot for Forsyth's troops. Therefore, the colonel pulled back across the bridge to a low tableland two hundred yards south of the mission, leaving two troops, under Captain Ilsley, to tie down the Indians and cover the retreat. Forsyth also sent a messenger to General Brooke requesting that the Ninth Cavalry be sent after all.

The colonel made his move too late, however. No sooner had he reached his new position than he and his troops came under fire from three directions—from the bluffs to the east and west, and from the south. Forsyth was pinned down, and Captain Ilsley and his men were trapped.

After sending Lieutenant Preston to hasten the Ninth Cavalry, Forsyth had a Hotchkiss gun wheeled into position and began firing into the bluffs to the east. The colonel sent a skirmish line up the lower bluffs to the west, but the line was driven back.

Fortunately for Forsyth and his men, Major Henry and his buffalo soldiers of the Ninth Cavalry, with two more Hotchkiss guns, arrived soon afterward. They had been delayed by the extreme exhaustion of their horses; the animals were still suffering from the punishing, one-hundred-mile ride of the day before.

Major Henry's men were not in much better condition than were their horses, but he deployed them swiftly. He sent a mounted skirmish line and a Hotchkiss gun up the steep east slope, and a dismounted line up the bluff to the west. With four Hotchkiss guns now clearing a path, the troops advanced steadily and forced the Indians to retreat. No longer pinned down, Captain Ilsley withdrew his men and pulled back across the bridge.

The Indians decided they had had enough and returned to their camp. The troops arrived back at Pine Ridge at dusk.

The next day, December 31, 1890, General Miles entered Pine Ridge to assume personal direction of the effort to woo the fugitive Brules and Oglalas back to the agency. Furious over the way in which a peaceful resolution of the Ghost Dance conflict had been scuttled by the massacre of Big Foot's band, and blaming Forsyth for the battle, Miles relieved the colonel of his command of the Seventh Cavalry and issued orders convening a court of inquiry. The court was to investigate the questions of whether Forsyth had so placed his troops at Wounded Knee that they shot one another and whether his men had wantonly killed women and children. After a lengthy investigation, Forsyth was not only exonerated on both counts but awarded the Medal of Honor for heroism at the Battle of Wounded Knee Creek. Four years later he was promoted to brigadier general.

There is no doubt, however, that the massacre at Wounded Knee transformed a minor Indian uprising into the biggest military action since the end of the Civil War. As a result of the uprising, there were thirty-five hundred soldiers in the vicinity of the Pine Ridge Agency. Two thousand additional troops were stationed nearby, ready to move if necessary. The objective of this massive military force was the four thousand Sioux camped fifteen miles north of the agency on White Clay Creek. About a quarter of this number were warriors, some of them followers of Short Bull and Kicking Bear.

Within a few days of General Miles's arrival on the scene, he had positioned his troops so that the Indians were boxed into White Clay Valley. The general sent Brooke and his men out to form the western and northern parts of a circle around the hostiles, cutting them off from a return to the Stronghold. Troops under Colonel Eugene A. Carr closed in from the east and northeast. There was no way for the Indians to move except toward the agency.

Not until the afternoon of January 1, however, did the hostiles realize that they were completely hemmed in. Fifty restless and still angry warriors rode out that day onto the bluffs overlooking White River five miles above the mouth of Wounded Knee Creek. Unknown to the warriors, the Sixth Cavalry had passed down the valley and camped at the mouth of Wounded Knee. The warriors saw only the regimental wagon train of the Sixth Cavalry, making its way slowly down the valley on the other side of the river.

Splitting the air with war cries, the warriors galloped

joyously down the slope, crossed the icy stream, and attacked the wagon train. Captain John B. Kerr, whose K Troop was guarding the train, quickly corralled the wagons and opened fire. The Sixth Cavalry down the river, under Colonel Carr, heard the fire and dashed to the rescue. The warriors hastily scattered into the hills south of the river. Nine of them were killed or wounded. There were no casualties among the army troops, but a white man, a cook for the agency herders, was killed by a small party of Brule warriors as he rode toward the agency that afternoon.

One of Miles's first acts upon arriving at Pine Ridge was to throw up defenses around the agency to guard against an Indian attack. Trenches were dug and earthworks constructed. Two companies of the First Infantry manned the defenses, and artillery covered all the approaches to the agency.

General Miles hoped to avoid a fight, however. He was one of those men, unfortunately too rare, who understood Indian psychology. He knew that persuasion combined with a display of overwhelming force could bring the Sioux in peacefully. Miles kept the line of troops pulled tight around the Indians, causing them much uneasiness but not frightening them enough to stampede them. At the same time, Miles began sending letters to Red Cloud, Little Wound, Two Strike, and some of the other chiefs, promising them good treatment but emphasizing that, in return, they must do exactly as he told them.

Elements within the Sioux encampment were working in Miles's favor. The Oglalas had already begun to regret that they had fled the agency. By joining with the followers of Short Bull and Kicking Bear, they had branded themselves as hostiles. The word had a fearsome connotation for them. The Oglalas still retained painful memories of the period before their surrender, when the army was pursuing them and trying to force them onto the reservations. The Indians had an even more current reminder of what it meant to be labeled "hostile" by the army. In their midst were the shattered survivors of Wounded Knee.

The fact that the Indians were now dealing personally with General Miles was another element in the general's favor, for many of the Oglala leaders were acquainted with the white chief of soldiers. They had surrendered to Bear's Coat, as they called Miles, on the Yellowstone River in the 1870s. He was one of the few white men they had met whose word they could depend on. If Bear's Coat said that not a shot would be fired nor a hand raised against any Indian who did as he directed, the Oglalas knew that the promise would be kept. Red Cloud and the other Oglala chiefs were ready to surrender to Miles.

The Brules were of a different mind. They refused to consider surrender or to view their position as hopeless. They had no idea of the course they could or should take and did not seem to be giving it much thought. Their main objective seemed to be stubbornly to hold out on a day-to-day basis.

In council the Brule and Oglala chiefs argued bitterly over the question of surrender. Short Bull and Kicking Bear denounced the Oglala chiefs for even considering such a move. The Miniconjous' followers held back any families who tried to leave the camp. Tensions grew between the two tribes. Quarrels broke out. Two Indians were killed.

On January 3 five Oglala chiefs—Big Road, He Dog, High Hawk, Jack Red Cloud, and Little Hawk—managed to slip away. They spent several days at Pine Ridge in council with Miles. When they returned with promises of good treatment for all who came in, the Oglalas were strengthened in their determination to surrender. Even some of the Brules began to consider the possibility, and they relaxed their guard around the camp. On January 7 seventy Oglalas managed to sneak past the pickets and made their way to the agency. They informed Miles that more Indians would be coming. Their report was correct. Red Cloud himself appeared the next day. With him were his son, Jack Red Cloud, He Dog, White Hawk, and their families. Later that day seventy-five more Oglalas made their escape from the hostile camp.

Meanwhile, Young-Man-Afraid-of-His-Horses arrived at Pine Ridge. He and his band had been visiting the Crows in Montana for the past two months. When General Miles heard that this influential Oglala chief was on his way back home, he sent an officer to intercept the party at Newcastle, Wyoming, and put the chief on a train to rush him back to the agency. When Young-Man-Afraid-of-His-Horses reached Pine Ridge, Miles immediately sent him to the fugitive camp to use his considerable power to persuade the hostiles to surrender.

General Miles decided it was time to increase the military as well as the diplomatic pressure on the Indians. He issued orders that the troops surrounding the hostile camp should prepare to draw their cordon tighter. When word came to him from Young-Man-Afraid-of-His-Horses that the Brules had reluctantly decided to move their camp a little closer to the agency, Miles ordered General Brooke and his troops to move at the same time.

On the morning of January 10, the Brules began slowly to move up White Clay Valley, arguing all the way about the wisdom of what they were doing. Brooke and his men followed, though out of sight. The next day the camp moved a little farther, this time stopping at the Drexel Mission, only five miles from the agency. Brooke was right behind the Indians, but he was exercising extreme caution. He didn't want to stampede them again.

A hard core of Ghost Dance believers still opposed the surrender. It was they who were doing all the arguing and keeping the Brules wavering in their decision to go back to the agency. But the counterforces were stronger than the arguments of the dancers. Each morning when the Brules awoke, they found the Oglalas packing to move on and soldiers camped in their rear. Turning back would have meant a battle against overwhelming numbers of bluecoats. Against their will, the Brules were being pushed toward the agency.

The surrender came on January 15. It was just a formality,

since hundreds of families from the hostile camp had been streaming into the agency for days. Yet "it was a spectacle worth beholding," recalled one officer.

> They moved in two columns up White Clay Creek, one on each side, about fifty-five hundred [actually the number was less than four thousand] people in all, with seven thousand horses, five hundred wagons, and about two hundred fifty travois, and in such good order that there was not at any point a detention on any account. . . . The rear and right flank of this mass was covered during the movement by a force of infantry and cavalry deployed in skirmish order, and moved with a precision that was a surprise to all who witnessed it.

The Indians set up camp at the agency, their tents stretching for three miles on either side of White Clay Creek. Miles assigned Captain Ezra P. Ewers to take charge of the "prisoners of war" and ordered them disarmed. Only two hundred rifles were found. Miles knew this was not even close to the actual number of guns in the Indian camp. But the general also knew it was impossible to keep an Indian disarmed for long, and he didn't want another massacre. He said nothing. Gentle persuasion induced the Indians gradually to hand over their guns. By the end of January the number of surrendered rifles had risen to six hundred.

The general made one demand, however. As proof that the Sioux had given up the Ghost Dance, he asked for the formal surrender of Short Bull, Kicking Bear, and several other prominent dance leaders. They were to be held in prison until the passions on the reservations cooled.

The designated men came forward voluntarily. Kicking Bear, rifle in hand, faced Miles. It wasn't the first time the two men had met under such circumstances. Kicking Bear had surrendered once before to Miles, in 1877. For the second time, the Brule laid his rifle at the feet of General Miles. So ended the Ghost Dance uprising, the last important engagement between United States troops and the Indians.

Two weeks before, on New Year's Day, 1891, the carnage

on Wounded Knee Creek had been cleaned up. After the massacre on December 29, the troops had returned to the agency, leaving the Indian dead and dying where they had fallen. The next day a howling blizzard swept the Sioux reservations and continued for two days.

When the weather cleared, a burial party started for the battlefield. Paddy Starr, a civilian, had contracted with the military authorities to bury the dead Indians at two dollars a head. He had hired thirty men to help with the job.

A troop of the Seventh Cavalry went with the burial detail to protect them from the thousands of hostile Indians who had fled the agency upon learning the fate of Big Foot's band.

Also accompanying the burial detail were close to seventy-five Oglalas, led by Doctor Charles Eastman, who were anxious to learn if any of their wounded Miniconjou kinsmen had survived their wounds and the blizzard.

The party started out soon after breakfast. The sun was shining, but it was bitterly cold, and three inches of snow lay on the ground. They arrived at the battlefield shortly after noon. It was a grim sight. One or two pole skeletons of lodges, a few wrecked wagons, some shreds of charred canvas, and scattered pots and kettles marked the spot where the Indian village had stood. Everywhere there were snow-covered mounds of bodies—in the razed village, in the old council square, in the ravine.

The Oglalas immediately burst into sounds of mourning. Some sang death songs. "It took all my nerve to keep my composure in the face of this spectacle," Doctor Eastman wrote later, "and of the excitement and grief of my Indian companions."

This wild display of grief discomfited the whites. They regarded the Oglalas uneasily, as if expecting them suddenly to hurl themselves vengefully against those responsible for such an atrocity. Doctor Eastman quickly set the Oglalas to work searching the mounds of bodies for survivors.

It was a stomach-churning task. The bodies, torn by shrapnel and rifle bullets, were frozen in the positions in which they died. Most of the dead warriors were found lying near the council square, where the fight began, but the bodies of the women and children were found scattered for two miles from the scene of the encounter. While trying to escape, they had been shot by infuriated soldiers who were too inexperienced in Indian warfare or perhaps did not care enough to differentiate men from women and children. Paddy Starr later recalled that he found three pregnant women shot to pieces, another woman with her abdomen blown away, and a ten-year-old boy with an arm, shoulder, and breast mangled by an artillery shell.

Miraculously, a few of Big Foot's people had survived the holocaust and the following blizzard. Doctor Eastman found a blind old woman who had not been injured and who had found partial shelter from the blizzard beneath a wagon. He also discovered a little girl, about four months old, lying beside her dead mother. The baby was wrapped in a shawl and only mildly frostbitten. On her head was a cap of buckskin decorated with an American flag done in beadwork. The child was taken back to the agency, where she was adopted by Brigadier General L. W. Colby, commander of the Nebraska state troops. The Indian women in camp gave her the name "Lost Bird." The Colbys had the child baptized under the name of Marguerite and raised her as if she were their own.

Two other Indian children were found alive and were later adopted—one by George Sword, captain of police, and the other, the four-year-old son of Yellow Bird, by Mrs. Lucy Arnold, a schoolteacher among the Sioux who had known the boy's family before the massacre.

Several wounded Indians had sought shelter in Louis Mosseau's store following the battle. Some had died there. A few were still alive. The number of survivors found by the burial detail totaled seven.

The search for survivors was a traumatic experience for Doctor Eastman, a full-blooded Sioux who had adopted the white man's way of life. "All of this," he said, "was a severe ordeal for one who had so lately put all his faith in the Christian love and lofty ideals of the white man."

While the wounded were put into wagons and taken back to Pine Ridge, the burial detail set about its work. The men began to dig a trench on the hill from which the Hotchkiss guns had destroyed the Indian village. It took the rest of that day and part of the next to prepare the mass grave and gather up the corpses. When the bodies were stacked on the hill, a count was taken. There were 102 warriors and young women, 24 old men, 7 old women, 6 boys between five and eight years old, and 7 babies under two.

Some of the whites stripped the corpses of Ghost Shirts and other articles to keep as souvenirs. Then the frozen bodies were thrown without ceremony into the trench.

One observer said later, "It was a thing to melt the heart of a man, if it was stone, to see those little children, with their bodies shot to pieces, thrown naked into the pit." Perhaps this writer was more sensitive than the others who were present, for when the last body had been thrown into the trench, the burial party posed around the mass grave on Cemetery Hill and had their picture taken. Then they filled the trench and rode back to the agency.

Years later Black Elk, recalling the massacre at Wounded Knee Creek, declared:

And so it was all over. I did not know then how much was ended. When I look back now from this high hill of my old age, I can still see the butchered women and children lying heaped and scattered along the crooked gulch as plain as when I saw them with eyes still young. And I can see that something else died there in the bloody mud, and was buried in the blizzard. A people's dream died there. It was a beautiful dream.

The old, beloved Sioux way of life could not be brought back. It was gone forever.

BIBLIOGRAPHY

BOOKS

Mooney, James, *The Ghost-Dance Religion and the Sioux Outbreak of 1890*, 14th Annual Report of the Bureau of American Ethnology, 1892–1893, Pt. II, Washington, 1896.

Neihardt, John G., *Black Elk Speaks* (Lincoln: University of Nebraska Press, 1961).

Tibbles, Thomas Henry, *Buckskin and Blanket Days* (Lincoln: University of Nebraska Press, 1969).

Utley, Robert M., *The Last Days of the Sioux Nation* (New Haven: Yale University Press, 1963).

Vestal, Stanley, *Sitting Bull* (Norman: University of Oklahoma Press, 1957).

Vestal, Stanley, ed., *New Sources of Indian History*, 1850–1891 (Norman: University of Oklahoma Press, 1934).

ARTICLES

Eastman, Elaine Goodale, "The Ghost Dance War and Wounded Knee Massacre of 1890–1891," *Nebraska History*, 26 (1945), 26–42.

Fechet, Maj. E. G., "The True Story of the Death of Sitting Bull," *Proceedings and Collections of the Nebraska State Historical Society*, 2d ser. 2 (1898), 179–89.

Mooney, James, "The Indian Ghost Dance," *Collections of the Nebraska State Historical Society*, 16 (1911), 168–86.

Index